A JOHN CATT PUBLICATION

Oliver Lovell

SWELLERS

COGNITIVE LOAD THEORY
IN ACTION

IN ACTION
SERIES

EDITOR
TOM SHERRINGTON

WITH FOREWORD BY JOHN SWELLER
ILLUSTRATIONS BY OLIVER CAVIGLIOLI

A
WALKTHRUs
PRODUCTION

First Published 2020

by John Catt Educational Ltd,
15 Riduna Park, Station Road,
Melton, Woodbridge IP12 1QT

Tel: +44 (0) 1394 389850
Email: enquiries@johncatt.com
Website: www.johncatt.com

Opinions expressed in this publication are those of the contributors
and are not necessarily those of the publishers or the editors. We
cannot accept responsibility for any errors or omissions.

ISBN: 978 1 913622 23 7

Set and designed by John Catt Educational Limited

For Granny and Bob

SERIES FOREWORD
TOM SHERRINGTON

The idea for the *In Action* series was developed by John Catt's *Teaching WalkThrus* team after we saw how popular our *Rosenshine's Principles in Action* booklets proved to be. We realised that the same approach might support teachers to access the ideas of a range of researchers, cognitive scientists and educators. A constant challenge that we wrestle with in the world of teaching and education research is the significant distance between the formulation of a set of concepts and conclusions that might be useful to teachers and the moment when a teacher uses those ideas to teach their students in a more effective manner, thereby succeeding in securing deeper or richer learning. Sometimes so much meaning is lost along that journey, through all the communication barriers that line the road, that the implementation of the idea bears no relation to the concept its originator had in mind. Sometimes it's more powerful to hear from a teacher about how they implemented an idea than it is to read about the idea from a researcher or cognitive scientist directly – because they reduce that distance; they push some of those barriers aside.

In our *In Action* series, the authors and their collaborative partners are all teachers or school leaders close to the action in classrooms in real schools. Their strategies for translating their subjects' work into practice bring fresh energy to a powerful set of original ideas in a way that we're confident will support teachers with their professional learning and, ultimately, their classroom practice. In doing so, they are also paying their respects to the original researchers and their work. In education, as in so many walks of life, we are standing on the shoulders of giants. We believe that our selection of featured researchers and papers represents some of the most important work done in the field of education in recent times.

An *In Action* book about Cognitive Load Theory was right at the top of our original list and Ollie Lovell immediately came to mind as the ideal person to write it. He has made a very significant contribution to the education community via his blog, including the extraordinary weekly blog of 'Takeaways', and his superb Education Research Reading Room podcast. Whilst Ollie shares ideas on a wide range of topics, it was through his exploration of Sweller's CLT

5

that I first came across him. His direct contact with John Sweller throughout the writing process has added a degree of conceptual rigour but, importantly, it is Ollie's grounded experience as a practising teacher that really brings it alive.

Finally, in producing this series, we would like to acknowledge the significant influence of the researchED movement that started in 2013, run by Tom Bennett. I was present at the first conference and, having seen the movement go from strength to strength over the intervening years, I feel that many of us, including several *In Action* authors, owe a significant debt of gratitude to researchED for providing the forum where teachers' and researchers' ideas and perspectives can be shared. We are delighted, therefore, to be contributing a share of the royalties to researchED to support them in their ongoing non-profit work.

FOREWORD
BY JOHN SWELLER

To be useful, an instructional theory has many prerequisites. Two prerequisites are critical. First, the theory itself needs to be guided by our knowledge of human cognition – how we learn, think and solve problems. Second, the effectiveness of the theory's recommendations must be testable and to have actually been tested with positive outcomes using randomised, controlled trials. Cognitive load theory meets both of these requirements. It rests on a bedrock of largely uncontroversial assumptions about human cognitive architecture, especially the characteristics of working memory and long-term memory along with the intricate relations between them. That cognitive architecture has been used to generate novel instructional procedures that then have been tested for relative instructional effectiveness by comparing them with more conventional procedures. If a new cognitive load theory procedure results in better learning than the currently conventional procedure as indicated by randomised, controlled experiments, a new cognitive load effect has been found, resulting in a new instructional procedure based on our knowledge of human cognition and rigorously tested for effectiveness.

The research literature describes many such procedures conducted by many researchers from around the globe with all those procedures available to practitioners, but there is a universal problem. That research literature is written primarily for technically competent researchers, not for practitioners who for the most part have not been trained as researchers nor have the time to assess the research literature in between their busy teaching duties. This superbly written book resolves this issue.

I first met Oliver Lovell, who is a high school teacher, several years ago. He asked to interview me for publication on his blog. I receive far more such requests than I possibly can accommodate but he was unusual in that he seemed to have a considerable familiarity with the cognitive load theory literature. I readily acceded to his request and even more readily agreed to provide him with feedback on the subsequent cognitive load theory book he intended to write. That book, which you now are reading, was intended for practitioners, unlike the research literature.

Oliver Lovell is not just familiar with cognitive load theory, he is a brilliant writer with a skill in distilling complex concepts into readily intelligible prose. I wish I could write as well as he writes. Accordingly, I would like to recommend this book in the highest possible terms to all educators who wish to familiarise themselves with cognitive load theory.

John Sweller

10 July 2020

ACKNOWLEDGMENTS

Without a doubt, I owe my first and greatest acknowledgement for this book to the originator of Cognitive Load Theory itself, Emeritus Professor John Sweller. It was John's openness and willingness to engage with a passionate young educator in 2017 which led to our first discussion, and it was this discussion, and the interview I published based upon it,[1] that lead to the opportunity for me to write this book. John's generosity again exceeded my expectations in late 2019 when he accepted my request for him to be a critical friend to me throughout the writing process, delivering a level of guidance, and a quality of feedback, that I was absolutely blown away by.

Throughout the process, John has been clear and direct in his feedback, pointing out misconceptions I've had, misconceptions that readers would likely encounter, and offering practical and actionable advice at every turn. Often I would send John several thousand words at a time, and he would reply in a matter of hours with detailed, perspicuous, and perspicacious suggestions, each of which improved the book immeasurably. Without the level of support that John provided, there is absolutely no way this book would be as true and accurate a representation of Cognitive Load Theory as it presently is. The icing on the cake has been the generous foreword that John penned for the book, as well as the quotes he provides in support of it. I will be forever grateful to John for the time that he has contributed to this project, and I hope this book serves to bring his work to many more classrooms throughout the world, and for many years to come.

Secondly, I owe a great debt of gratitude to Tom Sherrington. I was both surprised and humbled that, when it was decided that a book summarising Cognitive Load Theory in practical terms should follow Tom's hugely successful *Rosenshine's Principles in Action*, Tom thought of me and believed that I would be up to the challenge. Throughout the review process, Tom has been an immense support, providing practical guidance and advice regarding how to improve this manuscript, make it more accessible to teachers, and bring out my own voice more strongly.

Alongside Tom, I would also like to thank John Catt Educational, and in particular Alex Sharratt and Jonathan Barnes, who have been incredibly

---

1. This is available at: https://www.ollielovell.com/pedagogy/johnsweller/

positive, professional, and flexible throughout the process. I recommend any teachers or educators out there with an idea for a good educational book or resource to reach out to JCE, I could not be happier with the process of working with them! It is also JCE who provided the connection with Oliver Caviglioli, who has completed the beautiful illustrations within these pages. I'm grateful to Oliver for his excellent work on this book, and his immense contributions to education and information design more broadly.

Many other people also contributed during the review stage for this book, each of whom generously offered their time to read through all or parts of the manuscript, and offer thoughtful advice. In this vein, thanks go to: Bronwyn Ryrie Jones for taking the time to make suggestions on the introduction. Sue Gerrard for engaging me with some stimulating conversations regarding the biologically primary/secondary distinction (a topic I plan to continue to explore further in future). James Mannion for exchanges on the teachability of domain-general versus domain-specific skills. Jay McTighe and Gabriel Palmer for thoughtful notes throughout, but particularly for their promptings to improve the clarity of distinction between the redundancy and the modality effects. Lyn stone for pointing out my inconsistent use of the Oxford comma, and other punctuation tips.

Reid Smith for suggesting the inclusion of a reference to Daisy Christodoulou's marathon example in the chapter on segmentation. Ben Thomas for assistance with art examples. Judy Hochman for her correspondence regarding relations between Cognitive Load Theory and *The Writing Revolution*.[2] Michael Pershan for fantastic suggestions on the worked example chapter (I eagerly await Michael's book on this subject!). Wendy Taylor for picking up some blind spots I had, helping me to clarify wording, and just generally being a fantastic support and a great community builder within my local mathematics teacher community. Bryn Humberstone for his impressively keen eyes on the goal-free effect and self-explanation chapters and the thoughts he provided (sorry Bryn, the triangles + triangles diagram is still in the form of triangles!). Thomas Firth and Tal Ellinson for invaluable thoughts and suggestions on the final page proofs.

Alexander Renkl for his astute feedback on the self-explanation chapter, and his engaging correspondences on self-regulation. Dylan Wiliam for his contribution that, 'intrinsic load is optimised by good curriculum sequencing, and extraneous load is minimised by good instructional design',[3] and for his

---

2. The best book that I have ever encountered on teaching students how to write.
3. Dylan asserts that this isn't a line from him originally, but it is nonetheless one that he brought to my attention.

contribution in the goal-free effect chapter by sharing why it is he thinks that Cognitive Load Theory is the most important thing for teachers to know. And particularly to Catherine Scott and Steve Dinham for their thoughtful reading of the final manuscript, and their continuous support and encouragement right from the early days of my teaching career. I also owe much to Catherine and Steve for helping me to establish the Education Research Reading Room podcast (Steve generously volunteered as the first guest), a project that has shaped my professional knowledge and career in ways I could have never imagined!

Finally, a massive thanks to my incredibly supportive family, Madeleine, Malcolm, and Elliott, and my wonderful partner Holly. It is from your love and support over many years that I have developed the confidence to take on a project like this one, and I'm so grateful to you for always encouraging and supporting me to chase my dreams.

Oliver Lovell

16 August 2020

TABLE OF CONTENTS

INTRODUCTION: Why is *Cognitive Load Theory* important for teachers? 15

How to read this book 16

PART I: The A, B, C, D, E, of CLT 17

Architecture: the cognitive architecture of human memory 18

Biology: biologically primary versus biologically secondary information 22

Categorisation: categorisation of intrinsic and extraneous load 24

Domains: domain-general versus domain-specific knowledge and skills 27

Elements: element interactivity, the source of cognitive load 29

Summarising the ABCDE of CLT 33

PART II: Optimise intrinsic load 35

When to optimise intrinsic load 35

How to optimise intrinsic load 39

Pre-teaching 39

Segmentation 44

Sequencing and combination 49

The expertise-reversal effect 58

PART III: Reduce Extraneous Load..61

When to reduce extraneous load..61

Hone the presentation..61

   Redundancy 61

   Split-attention 72

   Transient information...88

   Modality..94

Structure the practice 104

   Worked examples...104

   Self-explanation 119

   The goal-free effect..134

CONCLUSIONS: Cognitive Load Theory, where to from here? 147

INTRODUCTION
WHY IS COGNITIVE LOAD THEORY
IMPORTANT FOR TEACHERS?

It was some time around the end of January 2017 that, scrolling through my Twitter feed, I came across the following bold claim:

> *I've come to the conclusion Sweller's Cognitive Load Theory is the single most important thing for teachers to know.*[4] *– Dylan Wiliam*

When Dylan Wiliam tweets, teachers pay attention, and I was no exception. In the months following, prompted by this tweet and an exponentially growing interest, I voraciously devoured all I could get my hands on in relation to Cognitive Load Theory. I wrestled with the seminal text on the subject, Sweller, Ayres and Kalyuga's *Cognitive Load Theory.* I read Sweller's *Story of a Research Program*, in which he outlines the origins of the theory and its subsequent development. I read blogs, listened to podcasts, read academic papers and finally, in July of that year, I took a flight to Sydney to interview the man himself, John Sweller.[5]

Through all of this exploration, and once I'd managed to peel back the layers of academic terminology in which the core ideas seemed to be encased,[6] I realised that what lay beneath was an incredibly rich and powerful model that would come to fundamentally change the way I saw my teaching, and my students' learning. Where once I would see just blank faces and puzzled looks from my students, I began to see cause and effect between my actions and their learning. The sources of my students' confusion came more clearly into focus, as well as the actions I could now take to better support their learning.

---

4. Wiliam, D. (2017) *I've come to the conclusion Sweller's Cognitive Load Theory is the single most important thing for teachers to know* (Twitter) 27 January. Available at: https://twitter.com/dylanwiliam/status/824682504602943489?lang=en
5. Sweller, J. (2017) Personal communication. Available at: https://www.ollielovell.com/pedagogy/johnsweller/ also translated into French: http://explicitementvotre.blogspot.com/2017/10/entretien-avec-john-sweller-par-oliver.html
6. Intrinsic, extraneous and germane load; the randomness as genesis, borrowing and reorganising, and environmental organising and linking principle; the transient information, redundancy and modality effects (to name just a few examples).

One key reason that I and many others have found Cognitive Load Theory so helpful is that, unlike much other research in the field of education, Cognitive Load Theory has had a singular focus for the duration of its development, improving instruction:

> *The ultimate aim of cognitive load theory is to provide instructional effects leading to instructional recommendations.*[7]

Written under the guidance of John Sweller, who has generously read and provided feedback on every word, I hope this book provides both an accurate and actionable guide for teachers who don't have the time to wade through the research, to struggle with the jargon, or to jump on a plane and interview John Sweller themselves, this is *Cognitive Load Theory in Action*.

How to read this book

This book is divided into three parts. Part I is dedicated to the five principles that underlie Cognitive Load Theory. This is the most theoretical portion of this book, and it's where the foundational ideas of the theory are communicated. If theory isn't your thing and you're keen to jump straight into practical strategies, you may like to start with Parts II and III, which are focused upon providing practical advice on how to apply Cognitive Load Theory in your classroom.

For those seeking a deep understanding of the theory, a great approach would be to read this book from front to back, then come back and reread Part I. By doing this you'll build a mental framework of Cognitive Load Theory during your first reading of Part I, add concrete examples through your reading about the cognitive load effects within Parts II and III, then deepen your theoretical understanding by revisiting Part I.

Regardless of how you choose to read this book, I hope you find it both practical and enjoyable, and that you and your students benefit from it for many years to come.

---

7. Sweller, J. (2016) Story of a Research Program. *Education Review//Reseñas Educativas.* 23. p. 11.

PART I
THE A, B, C, D, E, OF CLT

Cognitive Load Theory can seem like a lot to get your head around. There are many components to it, and many of them – for example 'human cognitive architecture' – can sound rather intimidating at first. Without some sort of framework to guide us along the journey, we risk getting lost. To help us overcome this challenge, I've come up with a quick and easy way to remember the five pillars of the theory. In fact, it's as easy as 'A, B, C' (D, E!). These five key principles represent the foundational ideas that underpin the remainder of the book. They are:

- Architecture: The cognitive architecture of human memory

- Biology: Biologically primary and secondary information

- Categorisation: Categorisation of intrinsic and extraneous load

- Domains: domain-general versus domain-specific knowledge

- Elements: element interactivity, the source of cognitive load

These five principles work together to produce the **fundamental recommendation of Cognitive Load Theory**: In order to increase learning, **reduce extraneous load** and **optimise intrinsic load**.

> **The fundamental recommendation of Cognitive Load Theory: In order to increase learning, reduce extraneous load and optimise intrinsic load.**

If this doesn't make sense to you as yet, don't worry. The goal is that you'll fully understand the idea, and how to apply it in your own classroom, by the end of this book!

Architecture: the cognitive architecture of human memory

The three components of our memory system

Why is it that a newly qualified teacher feels overwhelmed in a classroom that an experienced teacher would manage with ease? Why is it that we can struggle to remember a quote we've just heard? Why is it that students forget to complete seemingly simple steps, such as rounding their answer at the end of a question, or including a full stop at the end of a sentence? Each of these questions can be answered once we have an understanding of the cognitive architecture of human memory.

There are three key resources that we all draw upon in order to think: the environment, working memory, and long-term memory.[8]

The environment represents everything outside of our minds, it is the internet, books, magazines, knowledge readily shared by others, and more. The key thing to know about **the environment** is that it is an **unlimited *external* store of information**.

Long-term memory is where all our memories are kept. This includes memories of life events (episodic knowledge), factual information such as country names (semantic knowledge) and memories of processes such as how to tie a shoelace (procedural knowledge). As far as researchers are aware, there is no limit to long-term memory that can be reached within a human lifetime. Therefore, **long-term memory** is an **unlimited *internal* store of information**.

In addition to the environment and long-term memory, we also have working memory. Working memory is the site of consciousness, the part of memory where all thinking takes place. Unlike the environment and long-term memory, the capacity of working memory is limited to somewhere in the vicinity of four to seven 'elements' of information.[9] In effect, there are only so many elements of

---

8. This model was first proposed by Atkinson and Shiffrin in 1968. The full model also includes sensory memory, which is less relevant to the current discussion. Atkinson, R.C. & Shiffrin, R.M. (1968) Chapter: Human memory: A proposed system and its control processes. In Spence, K.W. & Spence, J.T. *The psychology of learning and motivation (Volume 2)*. New York: Academic Press. pp. 89–195.

9. Cowan, N. (2001) The magical number 4 in short-term memory: A reconsideration of mental storage capacity. *Behavioral and Brain Sciences*, 24(1), 87-114. And Miller, G.A. (1956) The magical number seven, plus or minus two: Some limits on our capacity for processing information. *Psychological Review*, 101(2), 343.

information that you can juggle in your mind at any one time. Thus, **working memory** is our **limited thinking system**.

Humans draw upon the environment (unlimited), working memory (limited), and long-term memory (unlimited), in order to think.

These three memory components are related within the processes of learning, remembering, and forgetting. The following diagram represents *some* of the key interactions between the environment, working memory, and long-term memory.

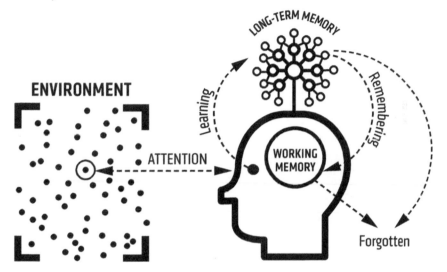

Learning and memory

As captured in the diagram, we reach out into the environment and bring new information into our working memory. Thinking about that new information and linking it to prior knowledge helps it to move from our working memory to long-term memory. In cases when this doesn't happen, information can fall out of working memory and be forgotten. Once in the long-term memory, we can 'remember' information as required, or, with insufficient use, we may lose the ability to retrieve it, and it is forgotten.

Working memory is the bottleneck of our thinking.

Because the environment is effectively limitless in scope, and our long-term memory is effectively limitless in its capacity, working memory – the only *limited* component of our memory system – acts as a bottleneck. Whenever we get confused, or feel like our head is going to explode from too many ideas, or struggle to follow along when we're reading something or someone is explaining it to us, it's because the limited capacity of our working memory is being overloaded. In Cognitive Load Theory, the words **cognitive load** represent anything that **takes up working memory capacity**.

Chunk and automate: how we think more complex thoughts

Given that our working memory can process only a limited number of elements of information at a time, how is it that we can think complex thoughts? The answer to this question relies upon the fact that not all 'elements' of information are created equal. The elements of information stored in our long-term memory increase in complexity over time, with smaller elements combining to form larger elements. The process of combining multiple smaller elements into a larger element within long-term memory is referred to as 'chunking', and it's what allows us to conduct more and more complex thought. This leads to a key finding of cognitive science, **that new information takes up more working memory capacity than familiar information**.

> **New information takes up more working memory capacity than familiar information.**

As an example, consider a child learning to read. A child who has not yet learned the alphabet will see the letter 'H' as three straight lines, three distinct elements of information. For them, reproducing these three lines in their correct relative positions – writing this letter 'H' which is new to them – could be a very cognitively demanding task. Over time, however, they'll 'chunk' those three lines as the familiar letter 'H' within long-term memory, and thinking about or drawing the letter 'H' will become automatic and effortless; a single 'element' within long-term memory.

Once this process of chunking abstract squiggles into letters is done for all the letters of the alphabet, they'll be familiar with each set of squiggles on a letter-by-letter basis, but whole words will still be new to them. A child will see the new word 'House' as a combination of five familiar elements; H, o, u, s, and e. At this time, combining these five letters will now become the cognitively demanding task. However, over time they'll further chunk the letters as the word 'House' in their long-term memory, and thinking about, reading or writing the familiar word 'House' will become automatic and effortless.

> **We reduce the working memory load of a task by chunking and automating.**

This process of **chunking** and **automating** continues on and on throughout life. This same child may grow up and write a novel, poem, or song about houses, and perhaps solve a riddle about them too, all the while working within the constraints of their limited working memory capacity. This is how the learning human is able to think more and more complex thoughts over time. We reduce the working memory load of a task by chunking and automating, the process of turning cognitively demanding new information into automated familiar information within long-term memory.

So, why do students forget to add a full stop?

We now have the knowledge required to answer the three questions with which we began this section on human cognitive architecture.

Why is it that a newly qualified teacher feels overwhelmed in a classroom that an experienced teacher would manage with ease?

The new teacher is overwhelmed because they are surrounded by new information, which **takes up considerable working memory capacity**. This is simply because the new information hasn't been chunked and automated yet.

Consider the task of closing a lesson. To close a lesson, the new teacher may think to themselves, 'Ok, to close I need to write a reflection question on the board, write out the homework, clean the rest of the board, hand students' homework books back, check the ground for litter, ask students to stand behind their chairs, and today I also have to remind them of the swimming carnival tomorrow'. That's a lot of elements to consider, and it's highly likely to overload their working memory, leading to one or more of the steps being forgotten. In contrast, the expert teacher would likely have the process 'close the lesson' chunked and automated in long-term memory as a single or reduced number of elements. They activate this automated 'close the lesson' procedure, and only have to recall one additional thing, 'Remember students, the swimming carnival is on tomorrow!' The experienced teacher handles effortlessly the same task that a newly qualified teacher finds completely overwhelming. They have chunked and automated.

Why is it that we can struggle to remember a quote we've just heard?

While we've probably stored in our long-term memory all the words that make up a new quote that we're keen to learn, the *new combination* of these words is likely to exceed our working memory capacity.

Why is it that students forget to complete seemingly simple steps, such as rounding their answer at the end of a question, or including a full stop at the end of a sentence?

If our students haven't as yet chunked and automated a new solution strategy in their long-term memories, or automated the process of writing, then by the time they get to the last step – round your answer, or add a full stop – it's likely that their working memory will be completely overloaded by the immediate task at hand. There simply isn't room in working memory for them to hold that final step 'in mind', and they forget to take what seems to be an incredibly simple final action.

Biology: biologically primary versus biologically secondary information

The second pillar of Cognitive Load Theory is the distinction between biologically primary and biologically secondary knowledge.[10] The distinction between these two types of knowledge was proposed by the cognitive developmental and evolutionary psychologist David Geary.[11] This model splits knowledge into two categories; knowledge that humans have evolved to acquire (biologically primary) and knowledge that has only become relevant to humans within the last few thousand years (biologically secondary).

Sweller and colleagues provide the following list of proposed biologically primary knowledge and skills:

> ... *knowledge that allows us to listen and speak, recognise faces, engage in basic social functions, solve unfamiliar problems, transfer previously acquired knowledge to novel situations, make plans for future events that may or may not happen, or regulate our thought processes to correspond to our current environment.*[12]

---

10. Within this book the terms 'knowledge' and 'skills' are used relatively interchangeably. As mentioned within the context of cognitive architecture, skills can be thought of as procedural knowledge. There is also no major distinction made between semantic and procedural knowledge within Cognitive Load Theory (though distinction between cognitive and sensorimotor skills can, at times, be relevant, such as in the case of the imagination effect).

11. Geary, D.C. (2007) Educating the evolved mind: Conceptual foundations for an evolutionary educational psychology. In J.S. Carlson & J.R. Levin (Eds.), *Psychological perspectives on contemporary educational issues* (pp. 1–99). Greenwich: Information Age Publishing.

12. Sweller, J., Van Merrienboer, J.J. & Paas, F. (2019) Cognitive architecture and instructional design: 20 years later. *Educational Psychology Review*. 1–32. p. 10.

As per Geary's theory, learning biologically primary knowledge is unconscious, fast, frugal and implicit (without conscious effort). More than that, 'we experience no discernible cognitive load in acquiring the necessary skills in ... any ... biologically primary area'.[13]

> **Geary suggests that we have evolved to acquire biologically primary skills and knowledge. They are learned automatically.**

In contrast, learning biologically secondary information is slow, effortful, and conscious. Some examples of biologically secondary information include the academic subjects taught at school and university, or how to operate a computer, car, or truck. In fact, it's argued that 'Educational institutions were invented because of our need for people to acquire knowledge of biologically secondary information.' and that 'Biologically secondary knowledge is knowledge we need because our culture has determined that it is important.'[14]

> **Geary's theory posits that biologically secondary skills and knowledge are only needed because culture suggests they are important. They are only learned slowly and with conscious and deliberate effort.**

Among many of the proponents of Cognitive Load Theory, the biologically primary/secondary distinction is drawn upon to make a case for what *should* be taught in schools based upon a belief of what *can* be taught in schools.

In essence it's argued that, because we've evolved to acquire biologically primary knowledge and skills, 'there is little evidence that they can be taught'[15] and therefore, we shouldn't bother trying. Sweller and colleagues build upon this to write:

> *Over the last few decades, many educationalists, correctly realising the importance of such [biologically primary] skills, have advocated that they be taught. Such campaigns tend to fail, not because the skills are unimportant but because they are of such importance to humans that we have evolved to acquire them automatically without instruction.*[16]

---

13. Sweller, J., Ayres, P. & Kalyuga, S. (2011) *Cognitive Load Theory*. Vol. 1. New York: Springer New York. p. 5.
14. Sweller, J., Van Merrienboer, J.J. & Paas, F. (2019) Cognitive architecture and instructional design: 20 years later. Educational psychology review. 1–32. p. 11.
15. Sweller, J., Ayres, P. & Kalyuga, S. (2011) *Cognitive Load Theory*. Vol. 1. New York: Springer New York. p. 8.
16. Sweller, J., Van Merrienboer, J.J. & Paas, F. (2019) Cognitive architecture and instructional design: 20 years later. *Educational psychology review*. 1–32. p. 10.

> **Prominent Cognitive Load Theory researchers suggest that instruction should focus on biologically secondary knowledge, because biologically primary knowledge cannot be taught.**

This is a controversial claim, and one that many readers will probably find challenging. If this is your feeling, you are not alone. In fact of the five ideas presented in Part I, it is the one around which there exists the most contention. For example, Geary invokes the idea that the human memory system is modular in its design as a basis for his theory, an idea that he himself admits is a topic of 'vigorous debate'[17] among researchers in the field.

Despite the debate surrounding Geary's distinction between biologically primary and secondary knowledge, all of the Cognitive Load Theory *effects* (to which Parts II and III of this book are dedicated) remain relevant and useful, and have been rigorously validated through randomised control trials. This book seeks to summarise the key ideas contained within the Cognitive Load Theory literature. Given the prominence of Geary's theory within the research, it forms an integral part of the work.

Categorisation: categorisation of intrinsic and extraneous load

Cognitive Load Theory's primary purpose is to work out how best to use the limited learning resource which constrains all human thinking; working memory. In the introduction to Part I, we learned that the fundamental recommendation of Cognitive Load Theory is to **reduce extraneous load** and **optimise intrinsic load**. This section provides the knowledge required to connect these two ideas, beginning with a definition of these two important terms.

Intrinsic cognitive load originates from the **nature** of the to-be-learned information. It is the cognitive load that is inescapable if the core to-be-learned idea is to be mastered, and it is what we want our students' working memories to be occupied with thinking about. For example, in order to be able to read, students must learn the relationship between the letter combinations printed on the page, and the sounds those letter combinations produce. There is simply no way around this. If we are teaching students to read, connecting letters and sounds is intrinsic to our goal.

---

17. Geary, D.C. (2007) Educating the evolved mind. In Carlson, J. & Levin, J.R. (Eds.), (2007) *Educating the Evolved Mind*. Charlotte, NC: Information Age Publishing. 1–99. p. 12.

> **Intrinsic cognitive load is the load associated with the core learning taking place; it is the load that we want students' working memories to be occupied with.**

In contrast, **extraneous cognitive load** originates from the **manner** and **structure** in which the information is presented to students. This is the cognitive load that teachers should seek to minimise. For example, while learning to read a child could get stuck on a word, and an adult could prompt them to consider the pictures nearby for clues. While this 'strategy'[18] may, in some situations, help the child to access the *meaning* of the sentence, it will not help the child learn to read. This is because reading requires connecting letters to sounds. Sound-letter combinations represent the intrinsic load, but including pictures is unrelated to connecting letters to sounds. The pictures are, therefore, extraneous to the goal of learning to read and can even hinder it.[19]

As a note of caution, this is not to say that images are always extraneous to learning, but in the case of learning to read, and referring to the images in a picture book to do so, they are. This highlights another key point: What is and isn't extraneous load depends entirely upon what the learning intention is. If, for example, our goal was not to teach reading, but rather to teach a particular *story*, pictures become very helpful indeed. In this new scenario, the pictures aren't helpful because they aid reading, they are helpful because they *bypass* the need to read by giving students access to the story's meaning via another channel.

> **Extraneous cognitive load comes from the manner and structure of instruction, and draws students' working memory resources away from the core information to be learned.**

Crucially, the *total* cognitive load a learner experiences is a combination of intrinsic and extraneous load. Put another way, intrinsic and extraneous load combined cannot exceed the capacity of working memory if learning is to occur. This explains why the core recommendation of Cognitive Load Theory is to reduce extraneous load and optimise intrinsic load. It is only by reducing extraneous load that we free up working memory resources which can then be allocated to increased intrinsic load, therefore increasing learning.

---

18. An excellent report on how these such 'strategies', including 'guess a word that would fit' are setting students up to fail can be found at: https://www.apmreports.org/story/2018/09/10/hard-words-why-american-kids-arent-being-taught-to-read

19. Torcasio, S. & Sweller, J. (2010) The use of illustrations when learning to read: A cognitive load theory approach. *Applied Cognitive Psychology*. 24 (5), 659–672.

> **Intrinsic and extraneous load combined cannot exceed the capacity of working memory if learning is to occur. In order to increase learning we must first reduce extraneous load to free up working memory resources, then allocate those now-free resources to intrinsic load.**

As such, **extraneous load** can be thought of as the '**froth**' of the learning task. At times, froth can be both enjoyable and helpful – a layer of insulation that tastes good and keeps the cappuccino hotter for longer, or a funny story about the teacher's experience that relates to the current topic. However, efficient instruction is achieved when froth is kept to a minimum, and **only included to the extent that it** *supports* **the primary learning goal.**

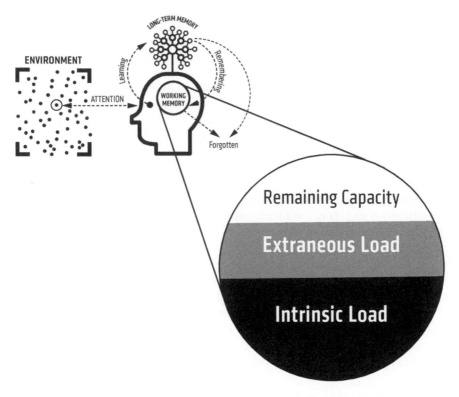

Working memory is occupied by a combination of intrinsic and extraneous load. The sum of the two cannot exceed working memory capacity if learning is to take place.

Domains: domain-general versus domain-specific knowledge and skills

We learned in the 'B of CLT' that the biologically primary versus biologically secondary distinction is drawn upon within Cognitive Load Theory to suggest that biologically primary skills, such as the ability to solve unfamiliar problems, can't be taught. This idea leads naturally to another important question, 'If we can't *teach* problem solving, how do people get good at solving problems?'

The answer lies in the 'D of CLT'. This 'D' stands for 'domain', meaning any field in which an individual can make the journey from novice to expert. Within this context, another key distinction within the Cognitive Load Theory literature relates to whether a skill is domain-general, or domain-specific (when 'skills' is used within this book it can be taken to mean both skills and knowledge, and vice versa).

Domain-general skills refer to general capabilities that are applicable, and widely transferable, across a broad range of tasks. The teaching of '21st Century Skills' or 'Enterprise Skills' – such as problem solving, creativity, communication, teamwork, and critical thinking – is founded on the assumption that these 'domain-general' skills exist, and can be taught, learned, and transferred.

In contrast, **domain-specific skills** and knowledge are only applicable within a specific domain, such as a certain branch of mathematics, classical literature, music theory, or chess. The knowledge of how to find the derivative of a function, play a musical scale, or move a knight across a board, are all domain-specific.

> **Domain-general skills refer to general capabilities that are applicable, and widely transferable, across a broad range of tasks. Domain-specific skills and knowledge are only applicable within a specific domain.**

Cognitive Load Theory places domain-general skills in the realm of biologically primary knowledge, whereas domain-specific skills are thought to be biologically secondary. Given this, it's argued that there is no need to teach domain-general skills because, 'we have evolved to acquire them automatically without instruction'.[20] This brings us back to our question about problem solving. If it's argued that domain-general skills can't be taught, how do proponents

---

20. Sweller, J., Van Merrienboer, J.J. & Paas, F. (2019) Cognitive architecture and instructional design: 20 years later. *Educational psychology review.* 1–32. p. 11.

of Cognitive Load Theory believe that people get better at problem solving, creativity, or critical thinking in an area like maths, music, literature or chess?

The answer provided by Sweller and colleagues is as follows: 'In any biologically secondary area, we can expect the major, possibly sole difference between novices and experts to consist of differential knowledge held in long-term memory.'[21] Put another way, the only way to get better at problem solving or critical thinking in maths, literature, or chess, is to *learn* more about maths, literature, or chess. The primary difference between novices and experts in a given domain is that experts possess a greater amount of relevant domain-specific knowledge.

> **The primary difference between novices and experts in a given domain is that experts possess a greater amount of relevant domain-specific knowledge.**

Let's consider the example of chess, a domain in which the origins of expertise have been closely studied.[22] Many believe that the key advantage grandmasters have is that they are able to think many more moves ahead than the novice. The reverse is actually the case. Rather than thinking many moves ahead, 'chess grandmasters [have] knowledge of chess board configurations and the best moves associated with those configurations'[23] stored in long-term memory. Whereas the novice must look at a board and slowly work through a variety of possible moves and likely consequences, the expert simply recognises the board position, and selects from long-term memory one of the several good moves that come to mind given that scenario. They have chunked and automated, and this is what allows them to make better decisions in shorter time, sometimes to the point of playing several games in parallel, all the while working within the limits of their finite working memory. In short, 'Novices need to use thinking skills. Experts use knowledge.'[24]

While in the above example we referred to the board positions and associated valuable moves that a chess expert has stored in their long-term memory, the same is true for experts in other domains. However, rather than board positions

21. Sweller, J., Ayres, P. & Kalyuga, S. (2011) *Cognitive Load Theory*. Vol. 1. New York: Springer New York. p. 21.
22. Chase, W.G. & Simon, H.A. (1973) Perception in chess. *Cognitive Psychology*, 4(1), 55–81.
23. Sweller, J., Ayres, P. & Kalyuga, S. (2011) *Cognitive Load Theory*. Vol. 1. New York: Springer New York. p. 24.
24. Sweller, J., Ayres, P. & Kalyuga, S. (2011) *Cognitive Load Theory*. Vol. 1. New York: Springer New York. p. 21.

and moves, we can more generally consider that an expert in a given field has a large collection of **situations** and **associated actions** stored in their long-term memory. Experts can usually also explain *why* these situation → action pairs make sense, re-derive them from foundational principles, and explain the mechanisms behind them. But the fact that these situation → action pairs have been chunked and automated in long-term memory is also crucial to expert performance at a high level in a given domain.

We can recognise these situation → action pairs in a variety of situations, and in each case, the expert **recognises** a situation and **executes** an appropriate action. For example, a writer may recognise that they would like to build suspense within a certain paragraph, so executes the writing strategy of shortening sentences. An improvising musician may recognise the key a song is in, and the mood of the audience, then execute a series of note combinations they know will fit well in the situation. An experienced stockbroker may recognise a pattern in a price chart and execute a trading algorithm they know has a high probability of being profitable. In summary, 'For real competence, we also must learn to recognise large numbers of problem states and situations and what actions we should take when faced with those states and situations.'[25]

Thus, Cognitive Load Theory's answer to the question, 'If we can't teach problem solving, how do people get good at solving problems?' is as follows. Just as you can't be a generic 'expert' in all things, you can't be taught to be generically 'creative' in all things, or a good 'problem solver' right across the board. Expertise is domain-specific and depends upon the knowledge stored in long-term memory that's relevant to a given domain. As the argument goes, the only way to improve an individual's expertise is to do so within a given domain, and to do so by increasing their knowledge in that domain.

Put simply, 'The purpose of instruction is to increase the store of knowledge in long-term memory.'[26]

Elements: element interactivity, the source of cognitive load

Why is some material more difficult to learn than other material? This is the question the final principle of cognitive load theory enables us to answer.

---

25. Ibid. p. 24.
26. Ibid. p. 24.

For any learning to take place, a number of elements of new information must be considered and related in working memory, and then incorporated into long-term memory. The more elements of new information that a student is required to think about – to process in their working memory – during a learning task, and the more complex the relations between these elements – the number of interactions – the more challenging the learning task will be. Within Cognitive Load Theory, the higher cognitive load associated with more elements and more interactions is referred to as 'element interactivity'. **Element interactivity is the source of all intrinsic and extraneous load**.

> **Element interactivity is the source of all intrinsic and extraneous load.**

Material that is *low* in element interactivity can be learned in total isolation. For example, a student could learn a single English to Polish translation, cat = kot, without learning any other Polish words. Similarly, a student could learn a single multiplication fact, $2 \times 3 = 6$, or the identification of a single country on a map, without learning any other multiplication facts, or any other countries. All of this material is low in element interactivity because it can be learned in isolation, and therefore imposes a low cognitive load.

Learning the name of a single country is a task low in element interactivity

Conversely, material that is high in element interactivity contains multiple elements that must be simultaneously processed for learning to take place. Consider a student learning to 'provide the coordinates of Poland' based upon the map pictured below.

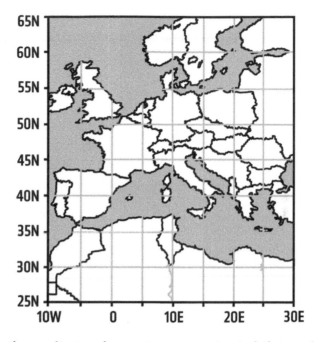

Finding the coordinates of a country on a map is a task that can be high in element interactivity

Let's look at a list of the *possible* elements of information a student would need to complete this task; they would need to simultaneously recognise and consider:

- Which of the outlines represents Poland.

- That coordinates are a set of two values, one giving latitude, one giving longitude.

- Latitudes are given by the numbers and letters on the vertical axis.

- The latitude of a location is found by tracing a horizontal line from that location to the vertical axis and recording the resulting letters and numbers.

- Longitudes are given by the numbers and letters on the horizontal axis.

- The longitude of a location is found by tracing a vertical line from that location to the horizontal axis and recording the resulting letters and numbers.

- An estimate must be made when the desired location exists between the latitude and longitude lines provided on a map.

- In writing the final coordinates, the latitude is written first and the longitude second.

While the answer is simply, 'The coordinates of Poland are 52°N, 19°E' a student with low prior knowledge could be required to simultaneously process the above eight elements of information to find the answer. This is a very cognitively demanding task and would likely overload their working memory capacity.

The phrasing, 'A list of the *possible* elements of information' is purposeful, because 'this number [of elements] is only an estimate based on the assumed knowledge of the learner.'[27] Importantly, the element interactivity of a task depends upon both the inherent nature of the task, *and* the background knowledge of the learner. If the learner already knows which outline represents Poland, that is one less element they must process during this learning task. If they already know that latitude is listed before longitude, that's another element which can be struck off the list. Taken to the extreme, for a domain expert who already knows where Poland is and knows how to find and represent coordinates, then there is only one element and the task becomes low in element interactivity.

As each of the eight elements in the above example are directly related to the task at hand, they are all elements that contribute to intrinsic cognitive load. If a task is too high in intrinsic element interactivity, it is the teacher's job to alter the learning intention to bring the task within the working memory limits of their students. In simple terms, **intrinsic load is optimised by appropriate curriculum sequencing**. Strategies to achieve this, such as pre-teaching, segmentation, and sequencing, are provided in Part II.

In other cases, there may be elements of the learning activity that are extraneous to the task at hand. In such a situation, it is the teacher's role to reduce these elements too. In short, **extraneous load is minimised by good instructional design**. This is the focus of Part III of the book, in which common sources of extraneous interacting elements, such as split-attention, redundancy, and transient information will be addressed.

---

27. Sweller, J. & Chandler, P. (1994) Why some material is difficult to learn. *Cognition and Instruction*. 12 (3), 185–233. p. 191.

> **Intrinsic load is optimised through appropriate curriculum sequencing, extraneous load is minimised by good instructional design.**

Cognitive Load Theory's instructional recommendations are directly aimed at altering the number of interacting elements within a learning task.

Summarising the ABCDE of CLT

So that's the ABCDE of CLT!

- Architecture: We think with a combination of information in the environment, long-term memory, and our limited working memory (the bottleneck of cognition). We overcome the limits of our working memory by chunking and automating information in long-term memory.

- Biologically primary versus secondary knowledge: David Geary proposed[28] that we've evolved to learn biologically primary knowledge without instruction, whereas biologically secondary knowledge, the focus of most schooling, must be taught.

- Categorising load as intrinsic or extraneous: Cognitive load is intrinsic if it results directly from the to-be-learned material, load related to anything else is extraneous. The key idea of Cognitive Load Theory is to minimise extraneous load and optimise intrinsic load.

- Domain-general versus domain-specific knowledge: One cannot become an expert in general skills like 'problem solving' or 'creativity' in all areas. Instead, we can only gain expertise in specific domains, and that expertise is gained by increasing our knowledge in that domain (which is often in the form of situation → action pairs).

- Element interactivity: Whether material is hard or easy to learn depends upon the number of intrinsic elements. The number of interacting elements depends upon the task itself, as well as the learner's prior knowledge. Intrinsic interacting elements are manipulated with good curriculum sequencing, while extraneous interacting elements are minimised through good instructional design.

---

28. Geary, D.C. (2007) Educating the evolved mind: Conceptual foundations for an evolutionary educational psychology. In J.S. Carlson & J.R. Levin (Eds.), *Psychological perspectives on contemporary educational issues* (pp. 1–99). Greenwich: Information Age Publishing.

It's a lot to take in, but hopefully the ABCDE mnemonic makes these ideas easier to remember. There remains, perhaps, one thing missing: a concise definition of Cognitive Load Theory itself! In a sentence: **Cognitive Load Theory is a series of instructional recommendations built upon knowledge of how humans learn**. We now turn our attention to these instructional recommendations.

> **Cognitive Load Theory is a series of instructional recommendations built upon knowledge of how humans learn.**

When to optimise intrinsic load

We learned in Part I that the core recommendation of Cognitive Load Theory is to reduce extraneous load and *optimise* intrinsic load. The fact that we need to optimise rather than simply *reduce* intrinsic load implies that, depending upon the situation, intrinsic load may need to be increased, decreased, or maintained. Let's consider a few such scenarios. We can do so with the aid of a 'bar model' that I have adapted from mathematics instruction to clearly represent the limitations of working memory, and the trade-off between intrinsic and extraneous load.

To begin, consider working memory as an empty box of limited capacity, as pictured below. As we know, this capacity is finite, and if exceeded, the student will experience cognitive overload and learning will be compromised.

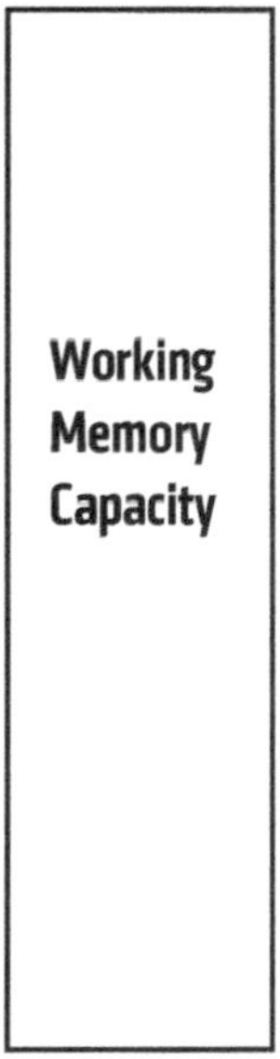

**Working
Memory
Capacity**

Standard instruction may look as follows, with working memory filled partially with elements that contribute to intrinsic load, and partially with elements that contribute to extraneous load, with a little capacity remaining:

**Standard
Instruction**

If we wanted to improve the effectiveness of this instruction, we would ideally reduce extraneous load (eliminating it would be ideal, but that's rarely possible), and increase intrinsic load in order to utilise the student's full working memory capacity for learning:

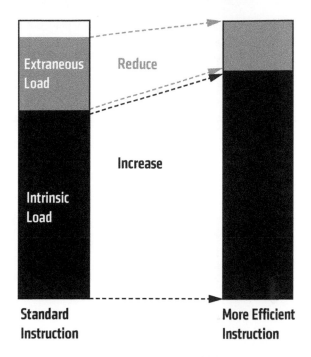

To make this idea more concrete, consider the following example of such a scenario. Students could be reading a book chapter about atomic models that includes an interesting but irrelevant sidebar detailing how Homer Simpson is a supporter of a sports team with an atom as its logo. This sidebar represents extraneous load, so if it were removed (or if students were taught to ignore it), this could free up working memory capacity dedicated to these extraneous details. This liberated working memory could then be allocated to intrinsic load, such as covering more of the chapter content.[29]

This represents a situation in which instructional efficiency can be improved by decreasing extraneous load and *increasing* intrinsic load. But the converse can also be true.

Imagine another scenario. This time, students are cognitively overloaded, perhaps they are being taught to find the latitude and longitude of Poland on the map, and they are overwhelmed by the complexity and difficulty of the task.

---

29. This study, students studying chapters on atomic chemistry with a sidebar on Homer Simpson as a supporter of the Springfield Isotopes, has actually been done! Bender, L., Renkl., A. & Eitel, A. (submitted) *Seductive Details Do Their Damage Also in Depleting Study Situations – When the Details Are Perceived as Relevant.*

The teacher may have already minimised extraneous load and really refined the instruction, but students may still be overloaded. In such a situation, the only way to make the task accessible to students is to *reduce* the intrinsic load, such as by segmenting the task – have students only find latitude first – or through other means as described in the remainder of this chapter. This can be represented pictorially as follows:

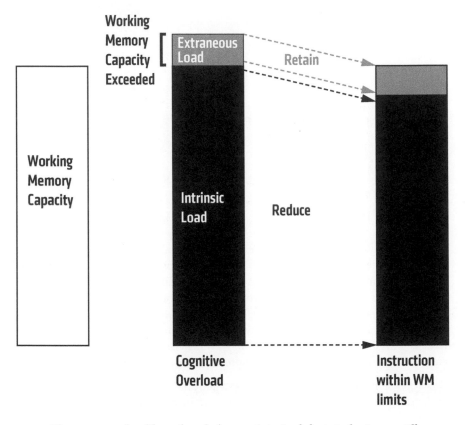

If extraneous load has already been minimised, but students are still experiencing cognitive overload, it is necessary to reduce intrinsic load to bring total cognitive load to within the limits of working memory.

There are other such examples that we could explore, but the underlying principle is the same. Our goal is to improve instruction, and this is achieved by first minimising extraneous load, then adjusting intrinsic load to ensure that our students' working memory capacity is fully utilised, without being overloaded.

Optimising intrinsic load isn't a precise science, we can't 'see' how full our students' working memories are in any direct manner. Despite this, by understanding that the goal is to minimise extraneous load, and optimise intrinsic load, we are better prepared to keep an eye out for signs that students are overloaded, or underloaded. The signs of overload (e.g., confusion) and underload (e.g., boredom) are already familiar to teachers. What is unique about Cognitive Load Theory is that it provides insight into the sources of overload or underload, and *instructional recommendations* for how to deal with them. We now turn to methods for optimising intrinsic load.

How to optimise intrinsic load

Pre-teaching

The idea of pre-teaching is a relatively simple one. If students experience high cognitive load when required to think about lots of *new* elements of information at one time (high element interactivity), we can reduce the cognitive load of the overall task by pre-teaching. Delivering a portion of the content before the main lesson, and reinforcing it through revision over time, can reduce the intrinsic load experienced by students when they attempt the final, complete task.

> **Delivering a portion of the content before the main lesson, and reinforcing it through revision over time, can reduce the intrinsic load experienced by students when they attempt the final, complete task.**

Pre-teach vocabulary

New vocabulary is a common source of high cognitive load for students, and it's been reported that if students don't know at least 90-95% of the words in a text, comprehension is severely diminished.[30] As such, pre-teaching the words that students are likely to encounter is an easy way to reduce the cognitive load of a reading task.

In his book, *Closing the Vocabulary Gap*,[31] Alex Quigley provides a methodology for explicitly teaching new vocabulary which is captured in the acronym SEEC: select, explain, explore, consolidate. Each of these steps could look as follows:

---

30. Nagy, W. & Scott, J. (2000) Vocabulary processes. In M.L. Ka-mil, P.B. Mosenthal, P.D. Pearson & R. Barr (Eds.), Handbook of reading research (Vol. 3, pp. 269-284). Mahwah, NJ: Erlbaum.
31. Quigley, A. (2018) *Closing the vocabulary gap*. Abingdon: Routledge.

In the context of pre-teaching, **selection** requires asking yourself questions such as:

- Which words will students need in the following lesson or topic?

- Which words are students unlikely to already know?

- Which words are likely to occur for our students across multiple subjects?

Explanation entails clearly pronouncing the word and giving the students an opportunity to say it multiple times, providing students with what Hollingsworth and Ybarra[32] refer to as a 'bullet-proof definition', and demonstrating some relevant examples. For example:

> New word: Absquatulate (Ab – squat – chew – late)
> Bullet-proof definition: To leave in a hurry
> Examples (it's good to provide several):
>> The student had to absquatulate when called by the principal.
>> The class absquatulated as soon as the bell rang.
>> 'Don't absquatulate, I still haven't given you your homework!' the teacher called out.

A good check for understanding at this point is to ask students to come up with their own examples to share with the class. Cold calling students (random selection of students to respond, often with the aid of pop-sticks) will aid you in uncovering common misconceptions regarding the word's appropriate use, which you can then address.

Quigley classifies **exploration** as an optional step, reserved for words of particular importance. Exploration can be achieved through:

- Considering the etymology (origins) of the world ('absquatulate' is a mid-19th century combination of 'abscond', 'squattle' or 'squat', and 'perambulate').

- Explaining or asking students for possible synonyms or antonyms.

- Creating a mnemonic for the world (imagine a person in the gym working out their abs, doing some squats, then leaving in a hurry because they're late for a date – absquatulate).

- Creating an image to associate with the word.[33]

32. Hollingsworth, J.R. & Ybarra, S.E. (2017) *Explicit direct instruction (EDI): The power of the well-crafted, well-taught lesson.* Thousand Oaks, CA: Corwin Press.
33. Fernandes, M.A., Wammes, J.D. & Meade, M.E. (2018) The surprisingly powerful influence of drawing on memory. *Current Directions in Psychological Science,* 27(5), 302-308.

Consolidation can be aided by systematic scheduling and prompting of students to use recently learned words in subsequent writing tasks.

Pre-teach characters

Have you ever read a book and become incredibly confused by the interconnected web of characters? This is a common challenge for students too. Who is related to whom, who hates whom, who is in cahoots with whom, it's a lot to keep track of! Each new character represents a new element that students must try to accommodate within working memory. Thus, pre-teaching characters can free up working memory resources to focus upon the details and nuance of the narrative. The benefits of pre-teaching characters are even greater for English language learners for whom the names themselves, let alone the characters to whom those names are attached, may represent new elements of information.

As Oliver Caviglioli expertly demonstrated in *Dual Coding With Teachers*, when it comes to communicating relationships between people and within organisations and structures, a diagram is often best.[34] In line with this, providing students with a character map, and having them learn it prior to reading the text, can significantly reduce the intrinsic load associated with reading.

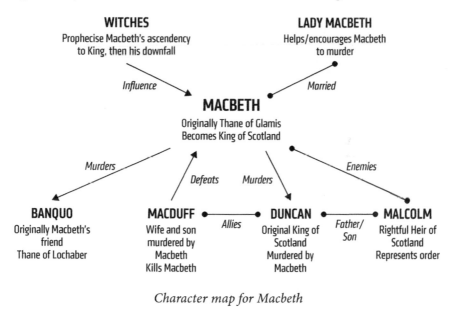

Character map for Macbeth

---

34. Caviglioli, O. (2019) *Dual Coding for Teachers*. Woodbridge: John Catt Educational. See the 'Modern Europe Project', p. 15.

A good classroom warmup while reading the book could be to have students working in pairs, with one student quizzing the other with questions such as, 'Who is the son of Duncan?' or, 'Who defeats Macbeth?' Ensure that students respond from memory, though they can use the character map as a scaffold in the early stages.

Pre-teach events and timelines

In history, and the social sciences more generally, students are often supported to explore 'big ideas' such as power, empire, or equality. This includes considering how these ideas have been manifested or interpreted through time, and in different locations. Understanding big ideas, and making historical connections, requires background knowledge that acts as the substance for such connections. Unfortunately, many students lack even basic knowledge of major historical events, making it impossible for such connections to be made. In such cases, pre-teaching can assist.

If teaching women's suffrage, a history teacher will likely want to highlight that women's wartime contributions played a role in changing the narrative in a way that led to many countries granting them the vote between the world wars. For many students, their previous learning about the two world wars might only be a vague memory, so spending a short amount of time re-visiting these ideas in the weeks or days prior to mentioning them in the context of female suffrage can help students to more securely relate these ideas in their memory.

In cases where pre-teaching by days or weeks is not possible, students can still be aided with the use of a simple timeline, pre-taught at the beginning of an activity. A powerful approach here is to draw up a simple timeline spanning the key decades or centuries, then give students a minute to silently write down from memory any events that may have happened within this time period, or a little outside of it, and to include dates if they can recall them. After students have retrieved all the events they can, take two to three minutes to add their contributions to the timeline, focusing upon the major events that the vast majority of students are familiar with (lest too many new interacting elements are introduced).

This activity is helpful in several ways. First, it provides an opportunity for students to retrieve from memory key dates; a valuable learning activity.[35] Secondly, it activates this prior knowledge and supports students to organise it in a way that forms a solid basis for connection with the new information that is to be presented.

---

35. Karpicke, J.D. (2017) *Retrieval-based learning: A decade of progress. In Cognitive psychology of memory, Vol. of Learning and memory: A comprehensive reference* (pp. 487–514).

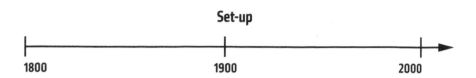

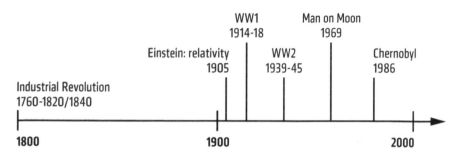

Timeline using students' prior knowledge

Pre-teach skills

We often require students to undertake a task that relies upon the application of some skill, or set of skills, to a new situation. If the skills themselves aren't securely locked in to students' long-term memories, trying to learn the new skills in tandem with applying them to a new scenario will lead to a very high intrinsic load.

Clarke, Ayers, and Sweller[36] tested this principle in the context of learning mathematics in conjunction with learning to use spreadsheets. One group learned how to do the mathematics and operate the spreadsheet at the same time, while the other was first trained in spreadsheet skills and only *then* were introduced to the mathematical content. They found that 'Students with a low-level knowledge of spreadsheets learned mathematics more effectively if the relevant spreadsheet skills were learned prior to attempting the mathematical tasks.'[37]

---

36. Clarke, T., Ayres, P. & Sweller, J. (2005) The impact of sequencing and prior knowledge on learning mathematics through spreadsheet applications. *Educational technology research and development.* 53 (3), 15–24.

37. Clarke, T., Ayres, P. & Sweller, J. (2005) The impact of sequencing and prior knowledge on learning mathematics through spreadsheet applications. *Educational technology research and development.* 53 (3). p. 22.

This same principle can be applied to any domain in which a skill must be applied to content that students find demanding in and of itself. Whether it's the operation of a calculator, mathematics skills or terminology,[38] how to use lab equipment, or how to effectively give a presentation,[39] novices will experience lower intrinsic load if the skill is taught prior to the requirement to apply it to challenging content.

Segmentation

Pre-teaching is one form of a much wider strategy for reducing intrinsic load, that of segmentation. If students are overwhelmed by too many new elements at once, it logically follows that intrinsic cognitive load can be reduced by breaking up the task into bite-sized chunks. Within the Cognitive Load Theory literature, this is referred to as the *isolated elements effect*. Sweller and colleagues write, 'for learners with low prior knowledge, there are considerable advantages to providing a [segmented] approach, where intrinsic load is considerably reduced by providing first a task with a lower level of element interactivity followed by a more complete task with higher levels of element interactivity.'[40] Some useful methods for segmentation are described below.

> Intrinsic cognitive load can be reduced by breaking up a task into bite-sized chunks.

Construct a skills hierarchy

In *Ten Steps to Complex Learning*, Jeroen Van Merriënboer and colleagues[41] highlight that at the heart of the segmentation process is the construction of a skills hierarchy. Skills hierarchies – which also apply to knowledge – make explicit the interacting elements which must be mastered before a student can achieve the intended goal, and empower a teacher to segment their instruction and teach each of the constituent skills in turn.

---

38. Sullivan, P. & Gunningham, S. (2011) A strategy for supporting students who have fallen behind in the learning of mathematics. In *Biennial Conference of Australian Association of Mathematics Teachers 2011* (pp. 719-727). The Australian Association of Mathematics Teachers (AAMT) Inc.
39. Mannion, J. & McAllister, K. (2020) *Fear is the Mind Killer*. Woodbridge: John Catt Educational.
40. Sweller, J., Ayres, P. & Kalyuga, S. (2011) *Cognitive Load Theory*. Vol. 1. New York: Springer New York. p. 216.
41. Van Merriënboer, J.J. & Kirschner, P.A. (2017) *Ten steps to complex learning: A systematic approach to four-component instructional design*. Abingdon: Routledge.

Skills hierarchies are best constructed by a true subject matter expert, and a good way to approach this is to have the expert complete the goal task from scratch, and to 'think out loud' while doing so. This process can even be video recorded and act as a stimulus for deeper review and consideration.[42]

In *Reflect, Expect, Check, Explain*,[43] Craig Barton offers some additional advice on creating a skills hierarchy (a process he refers to as 'atomisation') for maths teachers. Craig suggests: referring to supporting curriculum documents that list 'prerequisite skills', exploring the freely available 'small steps' guidance such as that provided by White Rose Maths[44] (example below), or utilising the process 'write a line, leave a line'.

▐ Given a numerical input, find the output of a single function machine

▐ Use inverse operations to find the input given the output

▐ Use diagrams and letters to generalise number operations

▐ Use diagrams and letters with single function machines

▐ Find the function machine given a simple expression

Modelled on White Rose Maths' segmentation for the concept 'Understand and use notation'[45]

To 'write a line, leave a line', have the expert (which will likely be you) leave a blank line between each line of mathematics working, then have them go back and try to add additional details and steps in-between each of the existing lines. This approach may help to uncover some of the implicit skills and knowledge used within the problem solving process.

An incredibly popular resource that takes the idea of a skills hierarchy even further is the book *The Writing Revolution* by Judith Hochman and Natalie Wexler.[46] I have heard many newly qualified teachers lament that they were

---

42. Van Gog, T., Paas, F., Van Merriënboer, J.J. & Witte, P. (2005) Uncovering the problem-solving process: Cued retrospective reporting versus concurrent and retrospective reporting. *Journal of Experimental Psychology: Applied, 11*(4), 237.

43. Barton, C. (2020) *Reflect, Expect, Check, Explain.* Woodbridge: John Catt Educational.

44. More examples of schemes of learning can be found at https://whiterosemaths.com/resources/

45. This document can be found at: https://whiterosemaths.com/wp-content/uploads/2019/SoLs/Secondary/Year-7-Full-Autumn-Term-2019-20-1.pdf

46. Hochman, J. C. & Wexler, N. (2017) *The writing revolution: A guide to advancing thinking through writing in all subjects and grades.* New Jersey: John Wiley & Sons. See https://www.ollielovell.com/errr/judithhochman/ for a discussion with the author Judith Hochman.

never taught how to teach writing. In short, they have never seen the highly complex process of 'writing an essay', broken down into bite-sized chunks that they can instruct students in without overwhelming their working memories. Through the lens of Cognitive Load Theory, we can now see why Hochman and Wexler's book has taken the world by storm. It powerfully presents teachers with a skills hierarchy for writing, and provides structured exercises to scaffold students each step of the way. Below is a visual representation of one of the skills hierarchies contained within *The Writing Revolution* which looks at writing a topic sentence (TS).[47]

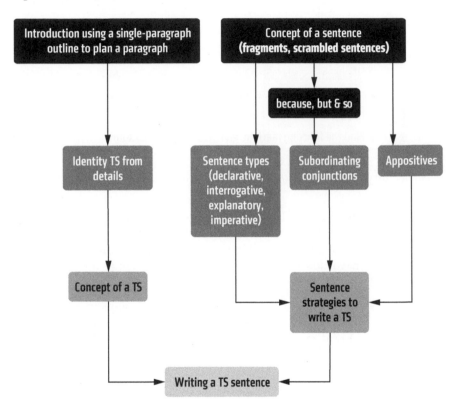

Skills progression towards writing a topic sentence, based upon
The Writing Revolution

---

47. Hochman, J. (2020) Personal communication.

One of the interesting implications of segmentation and progressive skill building is that, as Daisy Christodoulou writes, 'Complex skills are made up of many different elements and those distinct elements all look very different'.[48] What this means in practical terms is that, for complex skills, student practice of a segmented skill often looks very different from the final performance.

> **For complex skills, student practice of a segmented skill often looks very different from the final performance.**

While this idea is important in all subjects, it is particularly important for teachers of subjects involving lots of complex skills, such as physical education, art, and music. Christodoulou uses the example of marathon training to make the point. Although the goal of a practising marathon runner is to travel 42km in shorter and shorter times, segmentation doesn't simply mean to practice that overall 42km in chunks, but also to practice other exercises, such as body weight exercises, stretches, and weight training, that support the final performance in diverse important ways. A parallel in music could be the practicing of scales, or in art it could be simple but invaluable drawing skills exercises.[49] Effective segmentation for complex skills often requires practising a diversity of tasks that support, rather than directly underpin,[50] the final performance.

> **Department meeting idea**
> It's unrealistic to try to construct a skills hierarchy for every curriculum point, but it's likely that within your subject there are a few topics or skills that students seem to struggle with, year on year. For these few topics or skills, you may like to dedicate a department meeting to co-creating a skills hierarchy for one or a number of them. As well as being a valuable first step to improving the instruction of that topic or skill for students, it's also a great way to make the implicit knowledge of more expert teachers, explicit for those more novice. You may also find that the novices' questions prompt the experts to better dissect their own automatic and implicit thought processes!

---

48. Christodoulou, D. (2017) *Making good progress? The future of Assessment for Learning.* Oxford: Oxford University Press.
49. Some good activities for students learning to draw can be found at: https://drawinggym.co.uk/foundation
50. In slightly more technical terms, Christodoulou writes of how these training tasks such as the side-plank, weight training, flexibility, are probabilistically related to the final performance, rather than deterministically related.

Cut an element, or a few elements!

In some cases, the interacting elements of a task may be very easy to identify. For example, when playing the piano, the right and left hands must work in tandem, and a student must account for rhythm, tempo, and pitch all at the same time. In such cases, element interactivity can be reduced by simply subtracting one or more elements. This is something that music teachers often already do. They may have students clap the rhythm before playing it (cut out the element of pitch), practice the song at a slower speed and without a metronome (cut out the element of tempo), or practice the left and right hands separately prior to putting them together.

This can be done in other subjects too. In mathematics, if a student is learning the *algorithm* of double-digit multiplication, but they don't already know their times tables, expecting them to try to work out 9×6 during the process of multiplying 97×68 is likely to overwhelm their working memory. In such a situation, the elements associated with determining the single digit multiplication facts can be eliminated by providing students with a times tables grid, or ensuring that you only use numbers that will be easy for students to deal with, such as 23×32.

In English, if we're teaching students about the *structure* of a topic sentence, it's unnecessary to introduce additional interacting elements by expecting students to apply this structure to new content at the outset. First, teach the structure through the context of material for which they already have secure prior knowledge. Once the *structure* is stored in long-term memory, have them apply it to fresh content.

One final place we can consider the segmented introduction of elements is in the practice of concept mapping. Not long ago, at the end of a unit on magnetism, I printed out and cut up a series of images from the topic, about 30 in all, and asked my Year 12 physics students to use them to make a concept map detailing their relations. After a while, I noticed that one group in particular had barely started. They had about 15 of the pictures sitting in front of them, and they were just staring at them. They were feeling overwhelmed by the number of interacting elements!

I walked over, took all of their pictures and placed them face down next to their blank A1 sheet of paper. I then picked up just two and placed them face up and side by side in the middle of the sheet and said, 'Is there a connection between these two images? Discuss. I'll come back in a minute'. The students were immediately able to come up with a few connections and when I returned

I prompted, 'Turn one picture over at a time and try to connect it to one or more of the pictures already on your map.' It worked a treat! By cutting out all but two elements, the number of interacting elements was vastly reduced, and the students were able to progressively build up an interconnected network of the concepts, one interaction at a time.

Sequencing and combination

Sometimes when we break a complex task down into its constituent segments it will be immediately clear how best to sequence and combine them together again, while at other times, it won't be so obvious. One key decision to make at this juncture is whether to take a **part-whole** approach, or a **whole-part** approach. Part-whole means building constituent skills and knowledge before putting it all together. Whole-part requires providing a general overview first, followed by more focused practice of individual segments. There are benefits to each approach. In favour of the part-whole approach, Sweller and colleagues write, 'The initial presentation of part tasks helps consolidate procedures or rules, which can be applied to whole tasks at a later stage'.[51] In support of a whole-part approach, they add:

> *For complex motor tasks and many professional real-life tasks, it is essential that the learner understand and learn the relevant interactions and coordinations between the various subtasks. By learning the subtasks in isolation, these interactions may be missed.*[52]

Therefore, a part-whole approach can be effective when the individual segments of the task make sense in isolation, such as when teaching how to correctly use commas prior to having students apply them to a short writing piece. Conversely, when supporting students to take on a task such as writing a sonnet, it is imperative to start with an overview of the whole first, because it's the structure of the sonnet – typically 14 lines, with ten syllables in each, and a fixed rhyming scheme – which defines it.

> **Part-whole means building constituent skills and knowledge before putting it all together. Whole-part requires providing a general overview first, followed by more focused practice of individual segments.**

51. Sweller, J., Ayres, P. & Kalyuga, S. (2011) Cognitive Load Theory. Vol. 1. New York: Springer New York. p. 113.

52. Sweller, J., Ayres, P. & Kalyuga, S. (2011) Cognitive Load Theory. Vol. 1. New York: Springer New York. p. 114.

In the following, we will explore some methods for sequencing tasks from both a part-whole, and a whole-part perspective.[53]

Chain forwards or backwards (part-whole)

Forwards and backwards chaining, two concepts presented in *Ten steps to complex learning*,[54] is what we often do already when we sequentially present a set of skills or provide students with practice. The 'forwards' and 'backwards' refers to the order of practice of these different components.

Forwards chaining means progressively building a students' skills in the order in which they'll appear in the end product. A simple example is supporting students to write a science report, usually consisting of sections entitled: *Introduction, Hypothesis, Method, Results, Discussion, Conclusion*. A teacher could progressively support students to write a complete science report, bit-by-bit, through forward chaining. They could have students write an introduction for the first experiment or demonstration conducted in the classroom, a hypothesis for the second a few weeks later, a method section for the third, and so on. Then, once the students are confident with all the parts in isolation, they could combine them into a full science report at the end of the term or year. Forward chaining would work well with a science report, as such work follows a logical structure from start to finish.

> **Forwards chaining presents skills in the order in which they appear in the end product. Backwards chaining starts teaching with the last task in the skills sequence.**

Backwards chaining means getting students to work through the different parts of the overall task, but working backwards from the last task in the sequence. A common task in art and visual design is for students to put together a portfolio of their work, including annotations regarding their inspirations, thoughts, and reflections with reference to some stimuli. Students learning to do this task may benefit from backwards chaining. For example, the teacher could first provide students with an annotation template such as:

> *Date of encounter:*
> *Date of creation:*

---

53. This section draws heavily on Van Merrienboer, J.J. & Kirschner, P.A. (2017) *Ten steps to complex learning: A systematic approach to four-component instructional design*. Abingdon: Routledge.
54. Van Merriënboer, J.J. & Kirschner, P.A. (2017) *Ten steps to complex learning: A systematic approach to four-component instructional design*. Abingdon: Routledge.

Artist:

Medium:

Describe – What was the artist's intention, what did they do?:

Analyse – What do you think of it? Does it achieve its intention? Why does it work? Why not?:

Predict – Where could this go next? Has this made you think of anything else you want to explore?:[55]

Then have students fill it out based upon a stimulus image projected onto the board. The teacher could then provide students with a printed copy of the image for them to paste into their books. Finally, the teacher may run students through a discussion of ways to find inspiration, such as showing them some relevant parts of the library, directing them to some useful websites, or modelling how to view their surrounding world through an artist's eyes. Though students on their own will follow the process *search – paste – annotate*, the teacher has taught these skills in the reverse order *annotate - paste - search*.

Backwards chaining is particularly useful in this context because students will vary the most in their time taken to find inspiration. Some students will go outside, take three photos, and then be ready to paste and annotate. Others would spend 30 minutes in the library and still be looking for the 'perfect' source of inspiration. By starting with annotate and then paste, the teacher teaches these more discrete, time bound, and location bound skills first, then sets students off to explore.

Snowball (part-whole)

Snowballing[56] is a variation on forwards and backwards chaining that builds on the prior components each time. To return to our science report example, rather than have students complete one practical report segment with each new demonstration, teachers may instead 'snowball' the approach, having students complete the new segment, and all previous segments, each time.

Week	Demo or experiment in week 1	Demo or experiment in week 2	Demo or experiment in week 3	Demo or experiment in week 4	Demo or experiment in week 5	Demo or experiment in week 6
Task	Introduction	Introduction & hypothesis	Introduction, hypothesis & method	Introduction, hypothesis, method & results	(all prior) & discussion	(all prior) & conclusion \<this is a full report>

55. Thomas, B. (2020) Personal communication.

56. Van Merriënboer, J.J. & Kirschner, P.A. (2017) *Ten steps to complex learning: A systematic approach to four-component instructional design.* Abingdon: Routledge.

This is clearly a lot more work for students, especially if done with a time-consuming science report. If full-blown snowballing proves too demanding for students, the teacher could also semi-snowball the task, keeping the number of components to a maximum of three (or some other number) each time, as follows.

Week	Demo or experiment in week 1	Demo or experiment in week 2	Demo or experiment in week 3	Demo or experiment in week 4	Demo or experiment in week 5	Demo or experiment in week 6	Demo or experiment in week 7
Task	Introduction	Introduction & hypothesis	Introduction, hypothesis & method	Hypothesis, method, & results	Method, results & discussion	Results, discussion & conclusion	Full report

Why might a teacher snowball? Snowballing is useful if the skill building occurs over an extended period of time, or if the skill is one for which students require significant practice for mastery. The multiple exposures provided by snowballing give additional opportunities for students to embed each of the segments into long-term memory, and also space out the practice.[57] For example, in the semi-snowball approach above, students see each report section three times. This aligns well with the research of Graham Nuthall, who discovered that students require, on average, three engaged exposures to a concept in order to learn it. Amazingly, Nuthall and colleagues were able to use this simple 'three engaged exposures' heuristic to predict with approximately 80% accuracy the material that would, and wouldn't, be remembered by students.[58]

> **The multiple exposures provided by snowballing give additional opportunities for the students to embed each of the segments into long-term memory, and also space out the practice.**

Simplify conditions (whole-part)

A highly valuable real-world skill we often teach in school is oral presentation. Oral presentations include multiple components: gesture, intonation, pacing, phrasing, eye-contact, volume of voice, and, of course, the content of the presentation itself. However, the presentation is greater than the sum of its parts, and it makes little sense to ask students to practice each of these

---

57. Carpenter, S.K., Cepeda, N.J., Rohrer, D., Kang, S.H.K. & Pashler, H. (2012) Using Spacing to Enhance Diverse Forms of Learning: Review of Recent Research and Implications for Instruction. *Educational psychology review.* 24 (3), 369–378.
58. Nuthall, G. (2007) The hidden lives of learners. Wellington: Nzcer Press.

parts in isolation. A part-whole approach in this context is clearly absurd when we imagine a student standing at the front of class and practising *only* gesticulating, or *only* making eye contact, or *only*, speaking clearly and at an appropriate volume.

The useful way to reduce the intrinsic load of an integrated task like the oral presentation is to **simplify conditions**. Van Merriënboer and Kirschner describe this as follows:

> *In the simplifying conditions approach, the learner is trained in the execution of all constituent skills at the same time, but the conditions under which the whole skill is trained change and gradually become more complex during the training.*[59]

The way to simplify an oral presentation in this context is to have students begin to learn the integrated skills of an oral presentation in an incredibly simple context. This could mean having them present on a topic about which they're intimately familiar, or present one of several predefined famous speeches selected by the teacher. By simplifying the underlying task, students can rehearse the whole while reducing intrinsic load.

> **By simplifying the underlying task, students can rehearse the whole while reducing intrinsic load.**

The simplify conditions approach is applicable in a range of other domains also. Painting classes often start with simple objects such as an apple or a vase, so students are still required to integrate a whole host of skills, but the underlying stimulus is kept at a simple level to keep the task manageable.

This is also highly relevant for teacher training. Expecting newly qualified teachers to do everything – from researching the topic of instruction, to designing and writing a lesson plan, to running the final class with aplomb – is an immensely cognitively demanding task. Providing well-designed lesson plans for newly qualified teachers is one way to simplify the conditions of teaching, and allow them to focus on just the classroom delivery to begin with.

In science, ensuring that students know the likely outcome of a classroom practical activity prior to undertaking it is another example of simplifying conditions. If students have a firm grasp of the theory and likely outcomes of an experiment, they can focus more on the integrated procedure of it, such

59. Van Merriënboer, J.J. & Kirschner, P.A. (2017) *Ten steps to complex learning: A systematic approach to four-component instructional design.* p. 114.

as accurately completing the titration, or setting up their apparatus to reduce random errors.

Manipulate the emphasis (whole-part)

Emphasis manipulation is just a fancy way of saying, 'get students to focus on just a few key portions of the task'. This is another example of the *isolated elements effect*.[60] If a student really struggles with their spelling, a teacher may tell them, 'When I mark this essay, I won't be correcting your spelling at all, I'm only looking at the ideas that you communicate'. This allows students to complete the whole task of the essay while reducing the intrinsic load associated with worrying about their spelling.

In the mathematics classroom, a teacher could say, 'I'm not worried about whether or not you get the correct final answer when you do the following set of questions, what I'm looking at is whether or not you've substituted the numbers in correctly during the first step. Once we can all do that, we can focus more on the whole process.'

The science teacher may assert, 'I usually place a lot of emphasis on correct units, but in the following test I won't be assigning marks to units at all. Instead, I'll be focusing on your accurate use of significant figures.'

> **Emphasis manipulation, having students focus on just a few key portions of a task, is a powerful tool for reducing intrinsic load, especially in the early stages of integrating a new skill into an existing process.**

In each of these cases, the intrinsic load of a whole process such as write an essay, solve an equation or work out a problem, is being reduced by de-emphasising certain parts of it; the spelling, correct answer, or the units. Emphasis manipulation is a powerful tool, especially in the early stages of integrating a new skill – such as significant figures – into an existing process.

Introduce variation

We now have a range of powerful strategies to reduce the intrinsic load associated with a task. However, as our goal is to *optimise* rather than simply reduce intrinsic load, we also require methods to *increase* the element interactivity leading to intrinsic load. In fact, the reason for reducing extraneous load (as outlined in Part III) is to free up working memory capacity for increased

---

60. Sweller, J., Ayres, P. & Kalyuga, S. (2011) Cognitive Load Theory. Vol. 1. New York: Springer New York. p. 216.

intrinsic load, and therefore more learning! Adding variation to a sequence of tasks is one way to allocate free working capacity in a way that deepens learning.

The reason for reducing extraneous load is to free up working memory capacity for increased intrinsic load, and therefore more learning.

In the Cognitive Load Theory tradition, adding variation is often referred to as increasing 'contextual interference'. Here is how Sweller and colleagues describe it:

> *If problems are positioned next to each other in time and require the same set of skills for solution, then contextual interference is low. In contrast, if problems are positioned next to each other and require a different set of skills then contextual interference is high ... [De Crook and Colleagues[61]] ... found that learners who practised troubleshooting in a high contextual interference environment showed superior transfer skills than those who practised under lower interference. The advantage came at a cost. Students who practised under high interference conditions had delayed acquisition of the skill.[62]*

Students took longer to learn the skill because, by increasing variation (contextual interference), the number of interacting elements was increased. However, by providing more elements, so long as there is sufficient working memory capacity available to handle them, we also provide students with a greater opportunity to compare and contrast those elements, and to therefore build stronger connections. One of the easiest and most effective ways of introducing effective variation is through the process of interleaving, which essentially means 'mixing up' the practice instead of 'blocking' it all together.[63]

Increasing variation leads to deeper learning and increased transfer, but can slow down the learning process.

Here's how interleaving could be included into a sequence of work for mathematics. Imagine you're teaching students the formulas for the volume

---

61. de Croock, M.B., van Merriënboer, J.J. & Paas, F.G. (1998) High versus low contextual interference in simulation-based training of troubleshooting skills: Effects on transfer performance and invested mental effort. *Computers in Human Behavior, 14*(2), 249-267.

62. Sweller, J., Ayres, P. & Kalyuga, S. (2011) *Cognitive Load Theory.* Vol. 1. New York: Springer New York. p. 214.

63. Rohrer, D. (2012) Interleaving helps students distinguish among similar concepts. *Educational Psychology Review, 24*(3), 355-367.

of four different shapes: a wedge (W), a cone (C), a sphere (S), and a pyramid (P). Research shows[64] that the main challenge students have with this type of task is not *using* the formulas per-se, but rather working out which formula is most appropriate in a given situation. As such, it's less important that students' practice focuses on using the formulas, and more important that their practice focuses on *selecting* which formula to use. Formula *selection* practice can be achieved by presenting them with, for example, sixteen practice problems in random order (for example W-C-S-P-S-P-W-C-S-W-S-P-C-W-P-C), rather than in a blocked fashion (W-W-W-W-C-C-C-C-S-S-S-S-P-P-P-P). In fact, Dylan Wiliam recently suggested[65] that the one research paper he wishes all mathematics teachers would read is Doug Rohrer's freely available booklet on just this topic: structuring mathematics practice to give students opportunities to select appropriate solutions methods, and not just apply them.[66]

This approach also holds significant promise in other subjects, such as English as a Second Language (ESL). An ESL teacher who has recently taught their students simple past tense (SP), present perfect tense (PP), and the first (F), second (S), and third (T) conditional may be planning some practice for their students, and might have a set of questions such as the following:

> *Consider the sentence below.*
> *'I .... a car for my daughter last Christmas.'*
>
> *Select from the following options the word/s that best fill in the blank within this sentence:*
> *A. will buy*
> *B. have bought*
> *C. buy*
> *D. bought*[67]

If a teacher had fifty such questions, ten targeting each of the five grammar structures they'd just taught, it could be tempting to present them in the same

64. Rohrer, D. & Taylor, K. (2007) The shuffling of mathematics problems improves learning. *Instructional Science.* 35 (6), 481–498.
65. Wiliam, D. (2019) *Right now, it's Doug Rohrer and his colleagues' paper on interleaving in mathematics: http://bit.ly/2N07eou (pdf)* (Twitter) 9 September. Available at: https://twitter.com/dylanwiliam/status/1170840366729220096
66. Rohrer, D., Dedrick, R.F. & Agarwal, P.K. (2017) *Interleaving Mathematics Practice Guide.* Available at: http://uweb.cas.usf.edu/~drohrer/pdfs/Interleaved_Mathematics_Practice_Guide.pdf
67. Nakata, T. & Suzuki, Y. (2019) Mixing grammar exercises facilitates long-term retention: Effects of blocking, interleaving, and increasing practice. *The Modern Language Journal.* 103 (3), 629–647. p. 636.

order that the grammar structures were taught, such as SPx10, PPx10, Fx10, Sx10, Tx10. However, this approach is probably not as effective as presenting the questions interleaved or mixed up. While research has confirmed that students are likely to complete the work quicker under blocked conditions, and achieve more correct answers during practice, it won't prepare them as well for future scenarios in which they have to independently choose which tense to use, and how to apply it correctly.[68]

Interleaving has also been shown to be beneficial for native English speakers learning foreign languages. In one experiment, varying the verb conjugation practice for learners of Spanish led to more secure long-term learning than blocked practice of the same collection of different verb conjugations.[69]

Other realms in which interleaving has come to the fore include the teaching of chemical compounds in chemistry,[70] and distinguishing between the work of different artists in an art class.[71]

Two key caveats before we move on: firstly, interleaving helps learners to identify *differences* in situations where they have traditionally been confused by *similarities*. As we've seen, students often mix up different formulas, conjugations, or tenses. Therefore, interleaving holds most promise in these types of learning tasks. Second, the key danger associated with interleaving is progressing to interleaved examples too early. It's imperative that students can do each of the processes in isolation prior to them being interleaved. Remember, increasing variation increases intrinsic load, and should therefore only be used when there is spare cognitive capacity available.

> **Increasing variation increases intrinsic load, and should only be used when there is spare cognitive capacity available.**

---

68. The following examples are taken from, Nakata, T. & Suzuki, Y. (2019) Mixing grammar exercises facilitates long-term retention: Effects of blocking, interleaving, and increasing practice. *The Modern Language Journal.* 103 (3), 629–647.
69. Pan, S.C., Tajran, J., Lovelett, J., Osuna, J. & Rickard, T.C. (2019) Does interleaved practice enhance foreign language learning? The effects of training schedule on Spanish verb conjugation skills. *Journal of Educational Psychology.*
70. Eglington, L.G. & Kang, S.H. (2017) Interleaved presentation benefits science category learning. *Journal of Applied Research in Memory and Cognition.* 6 (4), 475–485.
71. Kornell, N. & Bjork, R.A. (2008) Learning concepts and categories: Is spacing the 'enemy of induction'? *Psychological Science.* 19 (6), 585–592.

The expertise-reversal effect

You may have noticed so far within this book that, whenever a new approach or strategy is presented, it's always presented with caveats. These caveats act as 'boundary conditions' for the instructional recommendation; advice about when it's likely to work, and when it's likely not to. Knowledge of boundary conditions is crucial because, without it, we're likely to apply an instructional strategy in an unsuitable context, or in an unsuitable way, leading to reduced learning.

One important boundary condition that stretches across all the cognitive load effects is the 'expertise-reversal effect'. Just as it sounds, **the expertise-reversal effect suggests that learners need differing amounts of support depending upon their level of expertise**. In fact, the instructional recommendations that Cognitive Load Theory provides for more novice and more expert students are often reversed.

> **The expertise-reversal effect suggests that learners need differing amounts of support depending upon their level of expertise.**

For example, novice students lack an understanding of how certain problems should be approached, and therefore benefit from worked examples, which provide a high level of guidance and structure. On the other hand, worked examples can be redundant for more expert students, who likely already understand how the problem should be solved. They therefore benefit more from *practice* rather than *examples* of problem solving. Problem solving provides the practice that these more expert students need to automate their skills. However, it provides insufficient support for novices who don't as yet understand the underlying procedures. The fact that worked examples are better for novices, and problem solving is better for experts, is the most commonly cited implication of the expertise reversal effect.

> **The fact that worked examples are better for novices, and problem solving is better for experts, is the most commonly cited implication of the expertise reversal effect.**

The difference between what's good for experts and what's good for novices can also be understood through our knowledge of element interactivity and the need to optimise intrinsic load. As we learned in Part I, the number of interacting elements present in a task depends upon the prior knowledge of the learner. Because an expert has more background knowledge than the novice, they will experience fewer interacting elements in their domain of expertise. In this way, a complex task that may be overwhelming for the novice may be completed with ease by the expert.

It is important to note that whenever we refer to 'more expert' and 'more novice' students, we are not speaking in a general sense. Rather, we are speaking very specifically about students being more or less expert in a specific domain, or even sub-domain of knowledge or skill, such as having more or less expertise in balancing chemical equations, writing a topic sentence, or throwing a javelin.

As the expertise reversal effect relates to both intrinsic load, and extraneous load, it will be continually referred to throughout the remainder of this book, and should be kept in mind whenever the 'best' instructional methods are being discussed in education. We can never categorically say that one educational approach is 'the best', without first considering – among other things – for whom it is best.

...

Part II focused upon methods for optimising the intrinsic load imposed upon students during instruction. In Part III we turn our attention to the most famous of the cognitive load effects, those targeting the reduction of extraneous cognitive load.

When to reduce extraneous load

When is it a good idea to reduce extraneous cognitive load? Pretty much all the time! In fact, 'Cognitive load theory has been concerned primarily, though not exclusively, with reducing extraneous cognitive load.'[72] It's important to also note that a teacher aiming to increase learning of key material would never aim to *increase* extraneous cognitive load.

The only time that a reduction of extraneous load may be unnecessary is if the intrinsic load of the task is low to begin with, that is to say, the task is too easy. In such a situation, it's unlikely that the sum of intrinsic and extraneous load will exceed the limits of the learner's working memory. However, such a situation is probably an indication that the learning task is not well suited to the learner, and they would likely benefit from something more challenging.

Hone the presentation

The cognitive load effects presented in this section offer a variety of ways to improve the presentation of information by reducing extraneous load.

Redundancy

It appears to me that the redundancy effect is the most quintessential of all cognitive load effects. If a key goal is to reduce extraneous load, then eliminating redundant information is a crucial step in achieving this. This is the simplest way I've come up with to summarise the redundancy effect, **eliminate unnecessary information and do not replicate necessary information**.

---

72. Sweller, J., Ayres, P. & Kalyuga, S. (2011) Cognitive Load Theory. Vol. 1. New York: Springer New York. p. 68

> The redundancy effect: eliminate unnecessary information and do not replicate necessary information.

The redundancy effect with text and spoken word

'The most common form of redundancy occurs when the same information is presented in different modalities.'[73] One example of this is when information is presented in both spoken and written forms simultaneously.

It's a common practice for presenters to provide written information on their slides and then to read out that information during the presentation. To conventional audiences, this represents the presentation of redundant information. Only one presentation format is needed, either the written words, or the spoken words.

Why does hearing spoken words at the same time as seeing them written inhibit learning? To answer this question, we must first gain a deeper understanding of human cognitive architecture. All language is processed within a dedicated portion of working memory that deals with language.[74] Whether the language enters this portion of working memory through the ears (spoken words) or the eyes (written words), it is still processed in the same place. This means that **when information is presented simultaneously in written and spoken form, both sources of information are vying for the same working memory resources, and therefore interfering with each other**. The conclusion; don't read from your slides!

> When information is presented simultaneously in written and spoken form, both sources of information are vying for the same working memory resources, and therefore interfering with each other.

This form of the redundancy effect has clear implications for language learning. As is the case more generally, language teachers often present written text to students at the same time as reading the same text out to them. Many language teachers believe the benefit of this approach is that it helps students to understand the connections between the printed letters and the correct pronunciation of the words. This is true, but only to a point. For example,

---

73. Sweller, J., Ayres, P. & Kalyuga, S. (2011) *Cognitive Load Theory*. Vol. 1. New York: Springer New York. p. 142

74. Baddeley, A.D. & Hitch, G. (1974) Working memory. In *Psychology of Learning and Motivation* (Vol. 8, pp. 47-89). Academic Press.

Jase Moussa's PhD[75] demonstrated that for the group of learners she worked with, their reading, writing, translation, and listening skills were more reliably improved through reading practice only, other than any other instructional method tested, including reading along with the teacher, and listening only.

These results can be partly explained by the redundancy effect, but are possibly also due to the fact that when students read information for themselves, they can do so at their own pace and revisit words they particularly struggled with. When a teacher paces the material by reading it aloud, students lose this self-pacing ability. There is also potentially a relationship between self-pacing and learner ability and motivation. These results demonstrating the superiority of students' self-paced reading were found with self-motivated university students, and may not hold to the same level with a less-motivated group of younger students with lower self-regulation and metacognitive abilities.

While the redundancy of presenting text and spoken information simultaneously is a well-established cognitive load effect, we should be careful in suggesting that a *read only* approach is the best for all audiences. There are many students for whom written text may not be suitable, such as those who are sitting too far away, or those with reading difficulties, or who may be sight-impaired. Further, there are many audience members for whom a spoken-only approach would not be particularly suitable either, such as audiences including hearing-impaired members. As with all the cognitive load effects, best results will be achieved by combining knowledge of the effects, and caveats, with knowledge of your individual learners.

The redundancy effect with images and written words

Another common form of redundancy is to present the same information in both written and pictorial form. A good example of this comes from Sweller and Chandler's research.[76] Their study included an experiment in the subject of biology, in which they presented learners with three different diagrams of the heart. In the first instance, they presented a simple diagram of the heart with only the required information, as pictured on the following page.

---

75. Moussa, J. (2008) *The impact of spoken English on learning English as a foreign language: A cognitive load perspective.* Lambert Academic Publishing.

76. Chandler, P. & Sweller, J. (1991) Cognitive load theory and the format of instruction. *Cognition and Instruction.* 8 (4), 293–332.

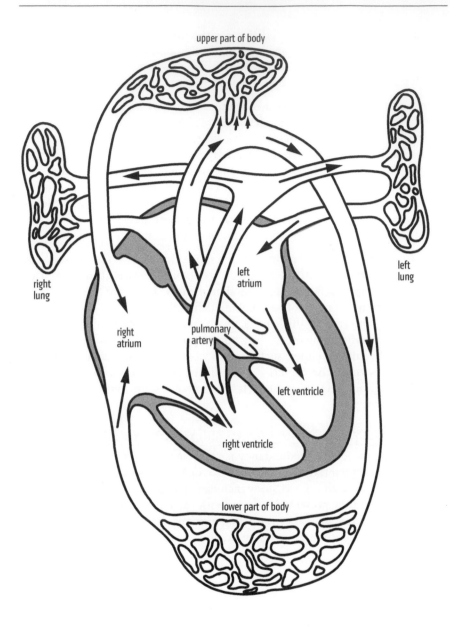

upper part of body

right
lung

left
lung

left
atrium

right
atrium

pulmonary
artery

left ventricle

right ventricle

lower part of body

Diagram with simple labelling

In the second instance, they added to the above diagram the following text:

1. *Blood from the upper and lower parts of the body flows into the right atrium.*

2. *Blood from the lungs flows into the left atrium*

3. *When the ventricles relax, blood from the right atrium flows into the right ventricle.*

4. *At the same time blood from the left atrium flows into the left ventricle*

5. *When the ventricles contract, blood is forced from the right ventricle into the pulmonary artery.*

6. *Blood is also forced from the left ventricle into the aorta.*

7. *The blood entering the pulmonary artery supplies the lungs.*

8. *The blood entering the aorta is pumped back to the body.*

This text was redundant because it re-stated information already contained within the diagram.

In the third case, the above text was integrated directly into the diagram, resulting in the following.

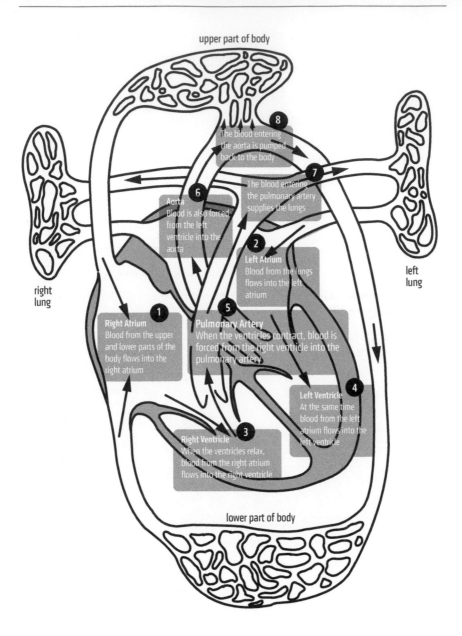

Diagram with additional, redundant labelling

Different groups of students were allocated to each diagram and then given as long as they pleased to study it. Once content, they then undertook six different tests, including labelling parts of incomplete diagrams of the heart, drawing blood flow on incomplete heart diagrams, and answering questions such as, 'Blood in the left atrium flows where?'[77] The tests were designed and balanced in such a way that they wouldn't favour a pictorial or written presentation of information.

In line with the redundancy effect, students presented with the simplest version of the instructions (the simply labelled diagram only) performed better than the other two groups in all six tasks, with five of these results reaching statistical significance. Even more impressive was the fact that students in the simple diagram group spent the shortest amount of time studying the diagram prior to testing, whereas the integrated diagram (diagram 3) group spent half as long again, and the diagram and text group spent more than twice as long.

Similar results were found by Bobis and colleagues,[78] who used the following instructions to teach a group of young children to fold a circle of paper into a triangular shape. Students presented with only pictorial instructions – the right-hand side of the image below – performed better than those presented with both the images and text.

77. Chandler, P. & Sweller, J. (1991) Cognitive load theory and the format of instruction. *Cognition and Instruction.* 8 (4), 293–332. p. 321.
78. Bobis, J., Sweller, J. & Cooper, M. (1993) Cognitive load effects in a primary-school geometry task. *Learning and Instruction.* 3 (1), 1–21. p. 6.

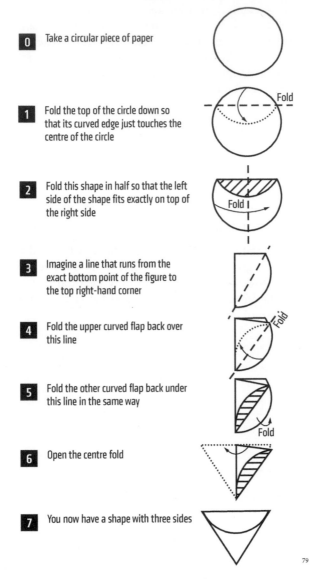

0 Take a circular piece of paper

1 Fold the top of the circle down so that its curved edge just touches the centre of the circle

2 Fold this shape in half so that the left side of the shape fits exactly on top of the right side

3 Imagine a line that runs from the exact bottom point of the figure to the top right-hand corner

4 Fold the upper curved flap back over this line

5 Fold the other curved flap back under this line in the same way

6 Open the centre fold

7 You now have a shape with three sides

Redundant written instructions with clear pictorial instructions for folding a circle into a triangle

79. Bobis, J., Sweller, J. & Cooper, M. (1993) Cognitive load effects in a primary-school geometry task. *Learning and Instruction.* 3 (1), 1–21. Pg. 6

As supportive teachers, we often want to provide highly detailed explanations to our students, feeling that the more detail we add, the better off they'll be. The redundancy effect challenges this assumption. The point here is not that images and text together are bad, but that **images and text together represent redundancy if they both communicate the same thing**.

> **Images and text together represent redundancy if they both communicate the same thing.**

Bullet-proof definitions

Taken more broadly, redundant information within lessons is anything that distracts students from the core to-be-learned material. The extraneous load that we as teachers impose upon our students often stems from this form of redundancy. When giving instruction, we often want to provide a highly detailed and in-depth explanation, providing the full picture to our students, or colouring it with additional interesting details, images, or fun facts. In reality, highly detailed explanations often overload our students' working memories in the early stages of learning. There is, of course, a time for this additional engaging information, but that time is not when the intrinsic load of the task is already pushing the limits of our students' working memories.

In order to align instruction to the core concept being taught, a useful strategy to consider is Hollingsworth and Ybarra's[80] *bullet-proof definition*. A bullet-proof definition is a one-sentence summary of the key concept or idea the teacher is trying to convey. Here are a few examples of bullet-proof definitions, some of which are inspired by Hollingsworth and Ybarra's sample lessons.[81]

> Science lesson: *Identify and communicate sources of experimental error.*
> Bullet-proof definition: *Experimental error is the difference between a measurement and its true value.*

> Art lesson: *Describe the contribution of Marcel Duchamp's 'Fountain' to 20th century art.*
> Bullet-proof definition: *Marcel Ducham's 'Fountain' (1917) was a standard urinal presented as an artistic work that prompted the fundamental question, 'What makes something 'art?'*

80. Hollingsworth, J.R. & Ybarra, S.E. (2017) *Explicit Direct Instruction (EDI): The power of the well-crafted, well-taught lesson.* Thousand Oaks, CA: Corwin Press.

81. More sample lessons can be found at: https://teach.educeri.com/lesson/

History lesson: *Analyse the causes of the Cold War.*
Bullet-proof definition: *The Cold War was a period of tense competition (1947-1991) between the United States and the Soviet Union (USSR) without direct war between the two powers.*

Economics lesson: *Describe the role of government in a market economy.*
Bullet-proof definition: *A market economy is an economy that allocates resources using the market forces of supply and demand.*

Geography lesson: *Analyse progress towards attainment of the Sustainable Development Goals.*
Bullet-proof definition: *The Sustainable Development Goals are 17 interconnected health, social, economic, and environmental progress targets that the UN hopes will be reached by 2030.*

Hollingsworth and Ybarra recommend that we commence a learning episode with a bullet-proof definition, have our students read it with us, and then recite it to each other from memory. The teacher then says something like, 'Let me show you what this means', and proceeds to facilitate deeper understanding through providing supporting evidence, examples, experience, experimentation or discussion of implications of this main idea. Each time the teacher introduces a new example, they explicitly relate it back to the bullet-proof definition so that the example and the core principle underlying it become firmly linked in students' memories.

When I mentor student teachers, I emphasise the importance of them being able to clearly answer two key questions prior to every lesson: 1. What will your students be able to do at the end of the lesson that they couldn't do at the start? 2. How will you know whether or not they can do it? Constructing a bullet-proof definition is one clear and actionable way to home in on the first of these questions, and to more easily consider the kinds of feedback we will need to elicit from students in order to check our success. Put another way, a bullet proof definition can help a teacher to identify what is, and what isn't, redundant in a given lesson.

Redundancy and the expertise-reversal effect

Redundancy occurs when the same information is available to students from more than one source at the same time, making one form of that information redundant. However, what is redundant for one learner may not be redundant for another. Given the relatively larger amount of relevant knowledge stored in the long-term memory of a more expert student, some of the instructional materials that act as support for the novice, will actually be redundant for the expert. This is illustrated through the following study.

Jiang, Kalyuga and Sweller[82] compared the efficacy of three presentation formats: read-only, listen-only, and read-and-listen, for Chinese students learning English vocabulary and sentences. Student learning was subsequently tested via a listening comprehension test. They found that, for Chinese *university* students who could already decode written English, the greatest learning was achieved through the read-only practice. For these students, listen-only practice was too fleeting, and read-and-listen practice was redundant as they already had these letter-sound connections stored in long-term memory.

However, for Chinese *high school* students with weaker decoding skills, the read-and-listen condition was preferable. For these novices, hearing the words spoken in tandem with reading them wasn't redundant, because without it they weren't able to effectively connect the text on the page to the sounds this text produced. Rather than being redundant, the spoken version of each word was in fact vital to developing their novice understanding.

This is one example of the expertise effect in relation to redundancy. What is redundant for an expert is not redundant for the novice, and instructional recommendations are reversed accordingly. In fact, 'The expertise reversal effect was initially predicted by cognitive load theory as a form of the redundancy effect'.[83]

In my discussions with John Sweller, he emphasised one common[84] misconception when it comes to the redundancy effect. Redundancy relates to unnecessary or replicated information being presented at a given point in time, such as the same information presented in written and spoken form, or written and pictorial form, simultaneously. What is *not* redundant is presenting that same information again to students at *another* time in the future. Providing students with multiple exposures to key information, especially when those multiple exposures are carefully spaced out over time, represents a fundamental strategy to building secure long-term memories.[85]

To return to the bullet-proof definition with which we began this chapter, the redundancy effect urges us to **eliminate unnecessary information and do not**

82. Jiang, D., Kalyuga, S. & Sweller, J. (2018) The curious case of improving foreign language listening skills by reading rather than listening: an expertise reversal effect. *Educational psychology review.* 30 (3), 1139–1165.
83. Sweller, J., Ayres, P. & Kalyuga, S. (2011) *Cognitive Load Theory.* Vol. 1. New York: Springer New York. p. 155.
84. Sweller, J. (2020) Personal communication, 10 June.
85. Carpenter, S.K., Cepeda, N.J., Rohrer, D., Kang, S.H.K. & Pashler, H. (2012) Using Spacing to Enhance Diverse Forms of Learning: Review of Recent Research and Implications for Instruction. *Educational Psychology Review.* 24 (3), 369–378.

replicate necessary information. In line with this advice, we should endeavour to keep the redundancy effect in mind in our classrooms, presentations, and writing (including our use of footnotes!).[86]

Split-attention

The split-attention effect is extremely simple. In fact, I've come up with a rhyming sentence to make it easier to remember, **'Information that must be combined should be placed together in space and time'**. During learning, students are often required to integrate multiple pieces of information in order to understand the full picture of the learning task. This integration takes up valuable working memory resources, so the easier we can make it for students, the better. Placing related information closer together in space and time makes it easier for students to integrate it, and therefore reduces extraneous cognitive load.

> **Split-attention effect: information that must be combined should be placed together in space and time.**

Keep information close together in space

The split-attention effect was first discovered when it was found that there were some worked example formats that didn't appear to be effective.[87] It was found that the reason these worked examples were ineffective was due to split-attention, and since then, a whole raft of research has been conducted into the split-attention effect. Here are some examples of split-attention versus integrated information, from a variety of subject areas. The majority of these are taken directly from empirical research studies. In all such cases, the integrated format led to better learning outcomes.

---

86. Prior to writing this book, it was my habit to use many more footnotes than you see in this book's current form. I significantly reduced the number of footnotes after receiving the following feedback from John Sweller on some of the initial page proofs for this book: 'Remember the redundancy effect. Readers assimilating this footnote are using working memory for something other than what you are teaching. Same goes for all footnotes – I never use them because they are either redundant or if they are necessary and induce split-attention.' – John Sweller, personal communication, April 21, 2020. I hope that this footnote about redundant footnotes in this chapter about redundancy does not constitute redundancy John!

87. Tarmizi, R.A. & Sweller, J. (1988) Guidance during mathematical problem solving. *Journal of Educational Psychology.* 80 (4), 424.

Split-attention in mathematics

The domain of geometry within mathematics is where much of the split-attention research has taken place. It is often customary for textbooks to have diagrams as a figure, and descriptions of angles placed in a separate text caption, as follows.

Split-attention format:[88]

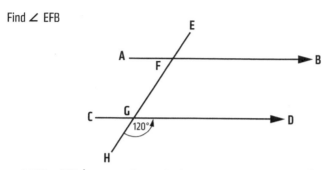

∠ GFB = 120° (corresponding angles between parallel lines AB & CD)

∠ EFB = 60° (angles on a straight line sum to 180°)

An integrated format, such as the following, reduces cognitive load.

Integrated format:[89]

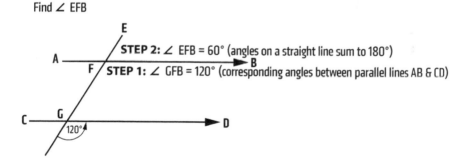

88. Sweller, J., Ayres, P. & Kalyuga, S. (2011) *Cognitive Load Theory.* Vol. 1. New York: Springer New York. p. 112.

89. Sweller, J., Ayres, P. & Kalyuga, S. (2011) *Cognitive Load Theory.* Vol. 1. New York: Springer New York. p. 112

In this worked example, it is demonstrated how to find the gradient of line NC. Split-attention format:[90]

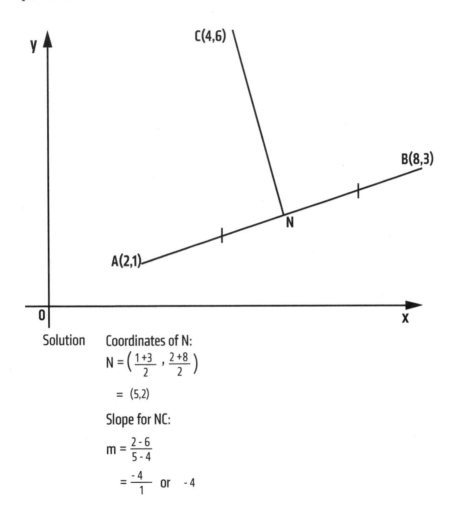

Solution   Coordinates of N:

$$N = \left(\frac{1+3}{2} , \frac{2+8}{2} \right)$$

$$= (5,2)$$

Slope for NC:

$$m = \frac{2-6}{5-4}$$

$$= \frac{-4}{1} \ \text{ or } \ -4$$

---

90. Sweller, J., Chandler, P., Tierney, P. & Cooper, M. (1990) Cognitive load as a factor in the structuring of technical material. *Journal of Experimental Psychology: General.* 119 (2), 176.

Integrated format:[91]

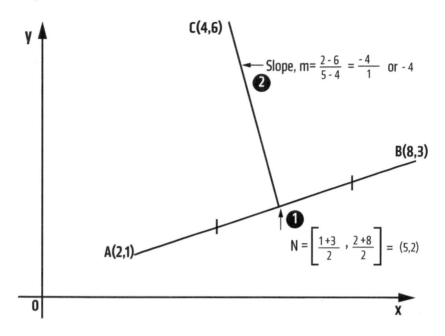

Split-attention in physics

For kinematics equations, it is customary to present the worded problem, and the working below it, inducing split-attention.

Split-attention format:[92]

> *A train moving from rest reaches a speed of 15 m/s after 5 seconds. What is the acceleration of the train?*
>
> *Working*

91. Sweller, J., Chandler, P., Tierney, P. & Cooper, M. (1990) Cognitive load as a factor in the structuring of technical material. *Journal of Experimental Psychology: General.* 119 (2), 176.
92. Sweller, J., Ayres, P. & Kalyuga, S. (2011) *Cognitive Load Theory.* Vol. 1. New York: Springer New York. p. 115.

$$u = 0 \text{ m/s}$$
$$v = 15 \text{ m/s}$$
$$t = 5 \text{ secs}$$
$$v = u + at$$
$$a = (v - u) / t$$
$$= (15\text{-}0)/5$$
$$= 3 \text{ m/s}^2$$

Once again, an integrated format for the worked example was shown to lead to increased learning for novices.

Integrated format:[93]

A train moving from rest (u) reaches a speed of 15 m/s (v) after 5 seconds (t) $[v = u + at, a = (v - u) / t = (15 - 0) / 5 = 3 \text{ m/s}^2]$. What is the acceleration of the train?

In this case, what is integrated is each pronumeral with what it represents. For example, novice students would likely miss the fact that the statement 'A train moving from rest' indicates that initial velocity, 'u', is equal to zero. By placing the pronumeral, 'u', next to the word 'rest', this reduces split attention for these novice students. This is similarly true to the final speed being 'v', and so on.

For an expert who already knows that 'moving from rest' means that '$u=0$', this integration presentation of the worked example is likely to be confusing, as the inclusion of the 'u', 'v', and other pronumerals in the original sentence represents redundant information (another example of the expertise-reversal effect).

Split-attention in chemistry

I recently observed a Year 8 science lesson on the periodic table. Each student had a copy of the periodic table in front of them, and the teacher had a slide similar to the following one displayed on the board.

---

93. Sweller, J., Ayres, P. & Kalyuga, S. (2011) Cognitive Load Theory. Vol. 1. New York: Springer New York. p. 115.

Learning to read the periodic table.

☐ Each box on the periodic table represents an element

☐ The atomic number gives the <u>number of protons</u> in the element

☐ The one or two letters in the middle of the box gives the element's <u>symbol</u>

☐ The word at the bottom of each box gives the element's <u>name</u>

Periodic table slide in split-attention format

She would read out one of the lines, then say, 'Can everybody find the symbol of an element on their periodic table?' Now, this teacher's instructions were very clear, and relating the description of an element on the board to a periodic table in a student's hand doesn't seem a particularly challenging task, yet some students were still getting lost. I could see their eyes darting back and forth between the board and their periodic tables, clearly struggling to integrate the text on the board with the table in front of them. This confusion was confirmed through my questioning of several students following the demonstration. This was a perfect example of split-attention inhibiting learning.

In the after-lesson discussion, we had a brief chat about the split-attention effect (I also mentioned redundancy) and brainstormed how these ideas could be taken into account to improve the lesson. We came up with the following.

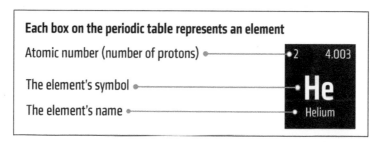

Periodic table slide in integrated format (with redundancy reduced)

This option cuts out redundant words, and visually integrates the required information.

Split-attention in second language learning

Second language learning often requires relating a foreign script to a foreign sound, and then to a word in the learner's native language. Lee and Kalyuga found that placing these three components in a way that made it clearer how the information was to be integrated, reduced extraneous load, and enhanced learning.

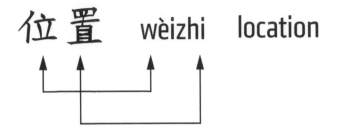

Split-attention format[94]

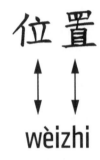

Integrated format

Split-attention in geography[95]

Purnell and colleagues studied the split-attention effect in geography. They compared a traditional split-attention map and an integrated format map to see which made it easier for students to learn key terrain features.

---

94. Lee, C.H. & Kalyuga, S. (2011) Effectiveness of different pinyin presentation formats in learning Chinese characters: A cognitive load perspective. *Language Learning.* 61 (4), 1099–1118. p. 1107.
95. Purnell, K.N., Solman, R.T. & Sweller, J. (1991) The effects of technical illustrations on cognitive load. *Instructional Science.* 20 (5-6), 443–462.

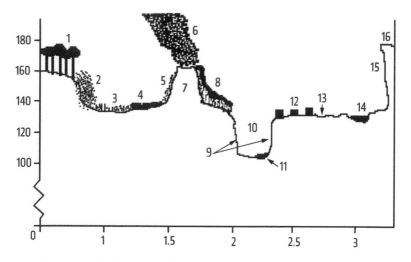

A cross section from macadamia nut plantation to Kola Resort

Key:

1. Macadamia nut plantation
2. Dense scrub
3. Maize
4. Wheat
5. Scattered scrub
6. Smoke and ash
7. Mt. Stellar (165m a.s.l. and 200m wide)
8. Woodland
9. Scattered scrub
10. Ford Canyon
11. Castle River
12. Cess Town
13. Rick Hwy
14. Lake Pierce
15. Joan's Cliff (43m high)
16. Kola Resort
Vertical scale: Height in metres
Horizontal scale: Distance in kilometres
Average gradient = 1:160

Split-attention format[96]

96. Purnell, K.N., Solman, R.T. & Sweller, J. (1991) The effects of technical illustrations on cognitive load. *Instructional Science.* 20 (5-6), 443–462.

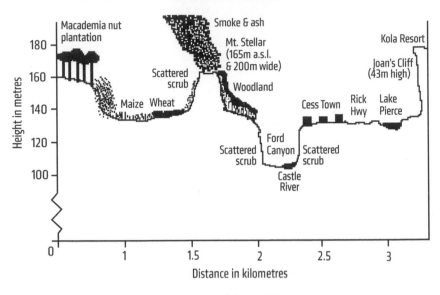

A cross section from macadamia nut plantation to Kola Resort

Integrated format[97]

The integrated format led to increased learning of the features.

Split-attention in music

When learning to play the piano, reading sheet music can be an incredibly cognitively demanding task. Students are trying to link the dots on the staves to notes, the notes to keys on the piano, then coordinate their fingers to play the appropriate keys at the appropriate time. This is a multi-step integration process that novices often find overwhelming. A video of a player's hands on the keyboard would reduce the amount of integration required to take place in the learner's working memory.

---

97. Purnell, K.N., Solman, R.T. & Sweller, J. (1991) The effects of technical illustrations on cognitive load. *Instructional Science.* 20 (5-6), 443–462.

Clair de Lune

from "Suite Bergamasque" L. 75

3rd Movement

Claude Debussy
(1862–1918)

Split-attention format[98]

---

98. Available at: https://musescore.com/classicman/clairdelune

HOW TO PLAY - Clair De Lune - by Debussy (Piano Tutorial Lesson)

Integrated format[99]

...

The examples are endless, but the point is that whenever students are required to integrate information in order to reach a complete understanding, cognitive load will be minimised by placing that information closer together, rather than further apart.

Another important place in which spatial split-attention is important is pagination. Pagination refers to how information is spread over a number of pages. When constructing learning resources, as well as tests and exams, it eases the extraneous load on students if all the required information for a given concept or question is contained within a single two-page spread. If students must flip back and forth between pages to integrate the required information, this will induce split-attention.

As with all Cognitive Load Theory effects, the cases in which a teacher will want to integrate information depends upon the desired learning outcome. In the music example above, if the goal for the novice learner is to learn the song 'Clair De Lune', they'll probably find it easier to learn through a YouTube video rather than sheet music. However, there may well come a time when they also

---

99. Amosdoll Music (2018) *How to Play – Clair De Lune – by Debussy (Piano Tutorial Lesson)*. Available at: http://tiny.cc/clairdeluneintegrated

want to learn to read sheet music, at which point the sheet music itself will no longer be extraneous. Similarly in the geography example, if the learning intention is to learn how to read a map's key, rather than learning the features of the terrain (as was the case in the example above) then including a key is intrinsic to the learning task and not extraneous.

Keep information close together in time

Students also experience the cognitive load of integration when information is split across time. This often happens when a verbal or written explanation is given prior to, or after, a demonstration.

Students are commonly faced with information split over time when receiving instructions. If, for example, a PE teacher tells her students, 'Ok, we're working through the fitness stations as follows. I want you to do ten push-ups at station one, 30 star jumps at station two, 20 crunches at station three, and 40 squats at station four', the fact that these instructions are provided prior to the actual activities increases the chance that students will forget. A better option would be to have a simple sheet of A4 paper at each station saying, for example, 'Station one: ten push-ups'. This approach integrates the instructions in time (and space) with the to-be-completed activity. A similar approach can be kept in mind for science teachers providing instructions in the lab, or any situation in which instructions are given. Place them as close in time and space as possible to the actual activity.

Another important source of split-attention that often compromises learning is excessive use of acronyms. When unfamiliar to a student, an acronym requires them to hold the meaning of the letter combination in working memory, or flip back a few pages, in order to double check the meaning. This is another example of split-attention. Acronyms should be avoided at all costs, unless you're absolutely sure that all students in your class can automatically understand their meaning (keep language learners in mind for this one in particular).

Similar to acronyms, using phrases such as, 'for the former', and 'for the latter', or 'the first', 'the second', and 'the third', can also induce split attention. Consider the following examples.

Split-attention format:

> *There are three key resources we all draw upon in order to think:* **the environment, working memory,** *and* **long-term memory.** *The first is an unlimited external store of information. The second is a limited internal store of information. And the third is a practically unlimited internal store of information.*

Integrated format:

> *There are three key resources we all draw upon in order to think: the environment, working memory, and long-term memory.* **The environment** *is an unlimited external store of information.* **Working memory** *is a limited internal store of information. And* **long-term memory** *is a practically unlimited internal store of information.*

In the split-attention example above, students must remember the three memory components (environment, working memory, and long-term memory) and their order if they are to link the components to their descriptions which are provided in the following sentences. This required integration produces extraneous load. The integrated format repeats each of the memory components directly next to their description, easing the burden on working memory.

While acronyms and expressions such as 'the former' and 'the latter' can tighten up writing and make it more time efficient for the author, they're usually done at the expense of the novice learner.

Split-attention, redundancy, and instructions

It seems only natural that, when supporting students to learn a new technology, whether it be a calculator, a computer, lab equipment, or a new tool in the technology room, students will be best off if given both a set of instructions, and the actual device itself to play with. However, research on the split-attention effect (combined with the redundancy effect), predicts, and has confirmed, that this is often not the case.

In this vein, Sweller and Chandler found that when a high-quality instructional manual was produced that contained all the information required to learn how to use computer-based spreadsheets (as shown below), students performed better when studying the manual only rather than learning with the manual and computer in tandem.[100]

---

100. Sweller, J. & Chandler, P. (1994) Why some material is difficult to learn. *Cognition and Instruction*, 12(3), 185–233. p. 207.

Computer Screen

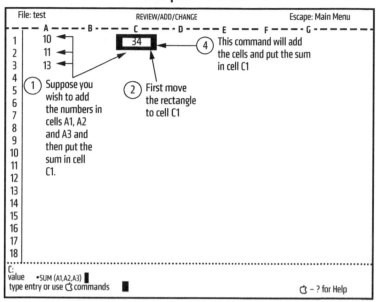

Computer Keyboard

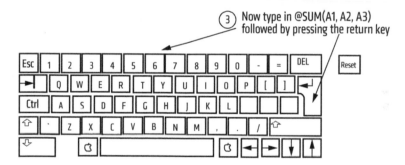

An image from the computer manual that integrated images of the computer with instructions regarding how to use it.

Further, students in the manual-only group took half the time to learn how to use the spreadsheet and computer compared to the group who had access to the computer as well (four and a half minutes versus nine). By integrating images into the manual, students weren't required to go between the manual and the instructions, mentally integrating the manual and the computer itself. As the integrated manual contained all the required information, the physical computer itself became redundant.

In the previous chapter we read of a study in which students were better able to complete a paper circle folding task when it included only pictures rather than pictures and redundant written instructions. The final experiment within this research study included a set of integrated instructions with the folding instructions *printed onto the circle itself!* Rather than reading instructions on an instruction sheet, then mentally integrating that with the circle of paper in their hands, the students simply followed the instructions integrated into the paper circle. Split-attention between the instructions and the paper had been totally eliminated, and students were more successful at the folding task.[101]

101. Bobis, J., Sweller, J. & Cooper, M. (1993) Cognitive load effects in a primary-school geometry task. *Learning and Instruction.* 3 (1), 1–21. Image from p. 16.

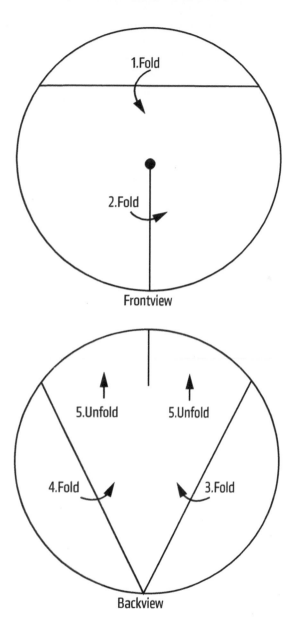

Images of the paper disc with folding instructions printed on it (integrated format).

The lesson here is that, in the early stages of learning to use a new technology, a highly efficient instructional method is to produce a concise manual that integrates informative images and descriptive text. Such an integrated format avoids the split-attention effect and, when created, can make the actual device itself redundant, such as in the computer spreadsheet example. One area in which this approach could be particularly beneficial is in preparing students for science laboratories. Students often become overwhelmed by all of the new apparatus, and a concise integrated manual that takes students through the practical prior to their encounter with the actual equipment could speed up the learning process.

In discussing this chapter with John Sweller, John highlighted a key misconception that teachers and researchers often form when first learning about the split-attention effect. They hear the advice that integrating information is good, and they begin to integrate *all* images and text within their instructional materials. This is a mistake. **Information should *only* be placed together in space and time if it can't be understood in isolation and is essential rather than redundant.** John describes this idea as follows, 'If a learner can't understand a diagram and text without considering both of them ("Angle ABC" is completely meaningless without the diagram), then they should be physically integrated. If the text just re-describes the diagram, physically integrating them will have negative consequences because it forces learners to read the redundant text.'[102]

> **Information should *only* be placed together in space and time if it can't be understood in isolation and is essential rather than redundant.**

The split-attention effect tells us that, in order to reduce extraneous cognitive load, **information that must be combined should be placed together in space and time.**

Transient information

When a teacher mentions a key point without writing it down for students, or flicks to the next slide while students are still frantically trying to remember what the previous slide said in order to write it down or apply it to a question, we are observing an issue caused by transient information. Transient information simply means information that is fleeting, here one second, and gone the next. Importantly, 'excessive cognitive load can be caused by transient information.'[103]

---

102. Sweller, J. (2020) Personal communication, 12 June.
103. Sweller, J., Ayres, P. & Kalyuga, S. (2011) *Cognitive Load Theory*. Vol. 1. New York: Springer New York. p. 220.

In summary, when information disappears, and students must therefore hold it in working memory, this causes extraneous cognitive load.

> **The transient information effect: when information disappears, and students must therefore hold it in working memory, this causes extraneous cognitive load.**

But transient information doesn't always impede learning. For transient information to cause a problem, 'Not only must the information be transient, it also must be high in information content'.[104] The transience of a simple spoken phrase such as, 'What is seven plus three?' won't cause a problem for most learners past the very early years of primary school. However, if you imagine trying to interpret the following spoken phrase by a physics teacher, 'Due to Lenz's law, the induced magnetic field within the copper coil will oppose the change in the initial magnetic field resulting from the movement of the bar magnet', it quickly becomes apparent just how taxing it can be for students to deal with informationally dense transient information!

This chapter offers strategies to reduce the cognitive load associated with transient information in our presentations, instructional videos, and during classroom discussions.

Transient information in presentations

Slideshows can be a useful presentation format, they allow the teacher to direct students' attention to different things at different times, they allow targeted pacing of information delivery, and they're also the accepted norm in many classrooms. But unfortunately, slideshows are one of the worst offenders when it comes to transient information.

Consider the following set of slides intended to teach punctuation.

---

104. ibid

Punctuation activity

Learning about punctation

Punctuation helps an author's writing to be easily understood.
Let's look at some common punctuation marks.

1

Punctuation: The full stop

Full stop

Rule: Use a full stop at the end of a sentence.
Example: I rode my bike to the shop.

2

Punctuation: The comma

Comma

Rule: Use an example to separate items in a list.
Example: At the shop I bought some oat milk, bread, broccoli, and vegan sausages.

Rule: Commas sit at natural pause points within a sentence.
Example: I like cats, especially those with big furry tails.

3

Punctuation: You try

You try: Complete the following by placing a comma or a full stop at the locations marked (once you're done, change the letter at the start of each new sentence to a capital)

*dogs are mammals that have been bred to live with humans_not in the wild_they have been bred by humans for a long time_and were the first animals to ever live with humans_ there are many types of dogs_such as beagle_retriever_Jack Russell_the dingo is also a dog_but many dingoes have become wild animals again_*

4

Teaching punctuation with transient information

The full stop and comma are clearly introduced, sure enough, but in the fourth 'you try' slide, all reference to what a full stop and comma is, or how they're used, has disappeared. This means that students must hold in working memory the full stop and comma definitions, at the same time as they try to apply this knowledge to the 'you try' question. This imposes a large cognitive load for students for whom the full stop and comma are novel information.

In this example, the problem of transient information could be remedied as follows:

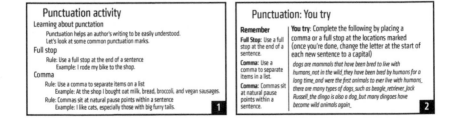

Teaching punctuation with reduced transient information

By having the small, 'remember' box on the activity slide, the key full stop and comma information is available for students' reference as needed. During the revised Slide 1 above, the text should be progressively revealed in order to manage students' cognitive load. This can be done in PowerPoint by selecting the text box, then selecting Animations → appear → text options → Group text: 5th level.[105]

Another way around this transient information effect is to provide students with printed or digital handouts of your slides. However, ensure that you provide this transience-reducing printout *only* when students need it, such as in tandem with Slide 4 in the first example above. Presenting it at the same time as the original slides would introduce redundancy.

Overcoming transient information in videos

Videos are another common source of transient information problems. If played for the whole class, individual students can't control the pace of the information flow, and are likely to become cognitively overloaded. However, several effective strategies have been developed to deal with this.

One option, in line with an idea from Part I, is to segment the information. Segmenting longer videos into comprehensible chunks provides breaks for students to process the information in-between segments, thus increasing learning.[106] Breaking videos into digestible segments also helps with student engagement. A study of 6.9 million instructional videos on Massive Online Open Courses (MOOCs) found that the median watch time for videos was six minutes, irrespective of the total length of the video.[107] That study's recommendation was to 'segment videos into chunks shorter than six minutes'.[108]

In addition to segmentation, providing learner control (such as offering stop, start, and pause buttons) can increase learning too.[109] Interestingly, this can

---

105. A video showing how to do this can be found at http://tiny.cc/pptanimatetext
106. Spanjers, I.A.E., Van Gog, T. & van Merriënboer, J.J.G. (2010) A theoretical analysis of how segmentation of dynamic visualizations optimizes students' learning. *Educational Psychology Review*, 22, 411–423.
107. Guo, P.J., Kim, J. & Rubin, R. (2014, March) How video production affects student engagement: An empirical study of MOOC videos. In *Proceedings of the first ACM conference on Learning@ scale conference* (pp. 41-50).
108. Guo, P.J., Kim, J. & Rubin, R. (2014, March) How video production affects student engagement: An empirical study of MOOC videos. In *Proceedings of the first ACM conference on Learning@ scale conference* (pp. 41-50). p. 42.
109. Mayer, R.E. & Chandler, P. (2001) When learning is just a click away: Does simple user interaction foster deeper understanding of multimedia messages? *Journal of Educational Psychology*, 93, 390–397.

improve learning even in cases in which the stop-start functionality isn't used![110] This could suggest that students learn better if they feel in control of their learning, regardless of whether they exercise that control or not.

A final recommendation for video presentations is to include pre-questions for students to attempt prior to watching the video. Importantly, it was found in one study[111] that pre-questions only provided a benefit if students actually *attempted* them; it didn't matter if they got them wrong, but simply reading the pre-questions didn't produce a significantly beneficial effect.

But beware, these globally positive pre-questioning effects seem to only hold for use with videos, and not for reading tasks. For videos, having students answer pre-questions can improve their retention of both the questioned and the non-questioned information.[112] Conversely, having students answer questions prior to a *reading* assignment does improve their retention of the pre-questioned information, but can act to *reduce* their retention of the non-pre-questioned information.[113] This could be due to the fact that, during reading, students can selectively skim the paper and only fully process the text that relates to the questions. This 'skimming' is not possible when students are watching an instructional video in full.

Overcoming transient information during classroom discussions

A final place where transient information is a consistent challenge for students is during classroom discussions. Particularly for English language learners, the fleeting nature of a comment made by a classmate or the teacher can leave students totally lost. Below are a few simple techniques to address this.

A tried and true method is simply to have yourself, or a student, write up on the whiteboard keywords representing contributions from different class members. These keywords, or short phrases, form something of a mind-map that helps to reduce the transience of the big ideas covered.

---

110. Hasler, B.S., Kersten, B. & Sweller, J. (2007) Learner control, cognitive load and instructional animation. *Applied Cognitive Psychology*, 21, 713–729.
111. Pressley, M., Tanenbaum, R., McDaniel, M.A. & Wood, E. (1990) What happens when university students try to answer prequestions that accompany textbook material? *Contemporary Educational Psychology*, 15(1), 27-35.
112. Carpenter, S.K. & Toftness, A.R. (2017) The effect of prequestions on learning from video presentations. *Journal of Applied Research in Memory and Cognition.* 6 (1), 104–109.
113. Carpenter, S.K. & Toftness, A.R. (2017) The effect of prequestions on learning from video presentations. *Journal of Applied Research in Memory and Cognition*, 6(1), 104–109.

Another strategy used by some practitioners of Philosophy for Children[114] (a method for facilitating meaningful class discussions) is to open up a text document, project it onto the board, and jot down in more complete form the contributions from different speakers during the conversation. While this is probably only possible for teachers with touch typing abilities (or by asking for the help of a student with such abilities), it can significantly reduce issues associated with transient information during classroom discussions. I use this strategy when cold calling student responses to 'explain' style mock exam questions. I will type up the first student's response, then cold call subsequent students and ask them for their thoughts on which parts of the response are the strongest, and which could be improved. I then edit the response in front of the group while actively manipulating the text on the screen. This form of answer refinement is much easier for students to follow than if the same refinement was simply done verbally.

...

Before closing this chapter, it's worth considering the difference between beneficial, and non-beneficial information transience. A time that a teacher may like to *purposely* make information transient is when supporting students to actively rehearse and retrieve that information from memory. For example, the teacher may show up a bullet-proof definition such as, 'The key recommendation of Cognitive Load Theory is to reduce extraneous load and optimise intrinsic load', then tell students that they are to mentally rehearse this phrase and tell it to their partner, and that they may be cold-called to repeat it. In such a scenario, the teacher removing the phrase from sight does not represent non-beneficial transience of information, but rather a deliberate strategy to prompt students to rehearse that information so that it begins to move from working, to long-term memory.

In cases in which the teacher isn't purposefully facilitating knowledge retrieval opportunities for their students, **when information disappears, and students must therefore hold it in working memory, this causes extraneous cognitive load.**

114. Gorard, S., Siddiqui, N. & Huat See, B. (2015) Philosophy for Children: Evaluation report and executive summary. *Education Endowment Foundation*, Millbank, UK.

Modality

When discussing the redundancy effect, we were introduced to the idea that **working memory has a portion dedicated to language processing**. This portion deals with all sounds and language, and we will refer to it as the auditory channel of working memory.[115] To understand the modality effect, it's necessary for us to be aware of the fact that **working memory also has a portion dedicated to image processing**, we will refer to this as the visual channel. Whenever working memory deals with anything to do with sounds or language, whether that information comes from the external environment or long-term memory, it is processed in the auditory channel. Whenever working memory deals with visual or spatial information, it is processed in the visual channel.

The 'modality effect' refers to simultaneously presenting related information via both visual and auditory channels, in order to take advantage of this 'dual channel' nature of working memory. As a result, the modality effect has two important benefits. Firstly, **by using working memory's auditory and visual channels in tandem, we can eliminate visual split-attention**. Secondly, **dual-channel presentation enables the processing of more information than via a single channel**.

> **The modality effect: present information via auditory and visual channels in tandem to eliminate visual split-attention and expand working memory capacity.**

Many people confuse the recommendations of the modality effect with the recommendations of the redundancy effect. Under redundancy, we found that we should *not* present written words and spoken words at the same time. But now it seems that we're being told the opposite! Not so. As is explained in more detail later in this chapter, the key difference is that with redundancy, written and spoken words are both vying for the same space in the auditory (language processing) channel of working memory. In the modality effect, the spoken words utilise the auditory channel, whilst the visuals occupy the visual channel. This distinction will become clearer throughout this chapter.

---

115. Baddeley, A.D. & Hitch, G. (1974) Working memory. In *Psychology of learning and motivation* (Vol. 8, pp. 47-89). Academic Press.

Using dual-modality to eliminate split-attention

Within our earlier chapter on split-attention, the key recommendation was, 'information that must be combined should be placed together in space and time'. However, when two pieces of to-be-combined information are both presented in visual form, irrespective of how *close* together we place them, it's impossible for them to be completely integrated. This is because there will always be a time delay between when the student looks at the first piece of information, and then looks at the next piece prior to mental integration. If, however, we take some of the information and speak it out loud so the student can hear it, we can now present the two pieces in a truly simultaneous fashion completely eliminating split-attention.

For our foreign language example presented earlier, this could look as follows:

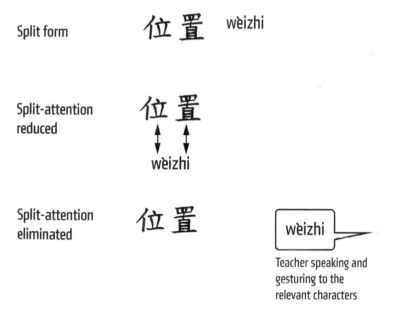

Thoughtful spatial design allows for the reduction of spatial split-attention, dual modality allows for its elimination

By pronouncing the mandarin word 'wèizhì' at exactly the same time as pointing to the characters wèi (位) and zhì (置), the teacher presents the information via the students' auditory and visual working memory channels simultaneously. By using two modalities, split-attention has been eliminated!

95

This same approach can be used for all the examples presented in the earlier chapter on split-attention, visual split-attention can be eliminated through judicious use of the modality effect. This is illustrated in the following:

From my classroom example, we previously reduced split-attention by presenting the periodic table as follows:

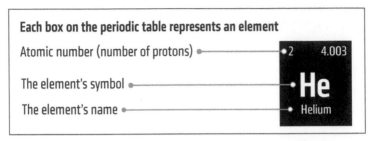

Classroom example of teaching elements with reduced split-attention

Split-attention could be *eliminated* if the teacher were to simply *project* up an image (visual) of an element of the periodic table on the board, point to the different components, and *say* (auditory) what each of them represents.

The same goes for learning from a map. Rather than reducing split-attention by writing the names of the different landmarks *on* the actual picture, the teacher could eliminate split-attention by *pointing* (visual) to each location and *saying* (auditory), 'This is Mt. Stellar' and, 'This is Joan's Cliff'.

In our 'Clair De Lune' piano example, the student could *keep their eyes* (visual) firmly on the video of the piano keyboard, and perfectly integrate the sounds that are being produced with the keys that they're seeing move.

Whenever teaching involves a concept that can be effectively communicated in pictorial form – a map, diagram, schematic, music notes, or a script during language learning – it's worthwhile considering using dual-modality instruction as a way to eliminate split-attention by utilising the full capacity of both the verbal and visual channels of working memory in tandem.

The transience trap when utilising the modality effect

But the modality effect faces several treacherous limitations. The first of which I have named the 'transience trap'.

If a teacher shows their class a diagram, and explains that diagram in spoken words, thereby utilising the modality effect, this is all well and good so long as the spoken information isn't too taxing. However, if the spoken presentation passes a certain threshold of difficulty for students, then the transient nature of the spoken word will begin to undermine the students' learning. In this way, the modality effect and the transient information effect are in tension.

The easiest way around this challenge is to present the information in dual modality format, but to include the explanation in written form for students' later reference (being careful not to introduce redundancy, see next section). If you use PowerPoint, you can write the description in the presenter's notes, then share the slides with your students after class. Another approach is to have your slides include only the image about which you plan to speak, but have the written explanation included in the handout. If you take this second route, ensure that when you're in the presentation phase you tell students to 'Close your books and look at me while I explain this. If you don't understand my explanation, you can re-read it on your handout later on, but for now, just focus on listening.' This approach has the added benefit of helping you to remember the explanation that you gave for a certain slide at a later date (you've written it down!), or supporting other teachers to interpret how you ran a class if they inherit your classroom resources in future. It also leaves students with an error-free record of a quality explanation which they can use to study independently later, reducing the need for them to frantically scribble down notes during your explanation, with the associated risk of them copying something down incorrectly and overloading working memory.

Personally, I usually teach from the same handout I provide to students (printed self-made booklets), and I usually include the written explanation alongside the image of a phenomenon. Given this format, when I project the booklet onto the board, I take advantage of the modality effect by simply zooming in on the section of the booklet that includes only the image. If there is still some text visible on the screen, I'll open up a blank text note (effectively a white box on my screen), and use it to hide any remaining text that may be distracting students from the image. The same can be done with a blank sheet of paper covering to-be-spoken text if you are using a visualiser.

Videos found online often fall prey to the transience trap. It is common practice for teachers to use videos from the internet in order to give a clearer demonstration of some visual phenomenon; from the growing of a plant, to the operation of some mechanical contraption, or the construction of a least-squares regression line. Unfortunately, it's unlikely that the original creator of the video took into account all of the cognitive load effects of which you're now aware. In fact, it's often quite the opposite, with many of the most popular YouTube content creators inserting enormous amounts of extraneous information into their videos, both visual and verbal, for entertainment purposes, and delivering *all* information at an exceedingly fast pace (the *Crash Course* educational videos are a good example of this).

In such cases, you may like to simply mute the video's original sound, and narrate over the graphics yourself. This gives you complete control over the amount of information presented verbally, and can help to reduce the overall cognitive load of the task while still taking advantage of the animations generated by the original presenter, and utilising the modality effect in doing so. If the video itself is still too fast-paced or 'busy', a further option is to screenshot a few key frames, and present them to students in static-pictorial form while you explain them. This enables you to utilise high quality images of key processes while controlling the complexity of both the visual and verbal presentation of information.

The redundancy traps when utilising the modality effect

Redundancy trap one: Simultaneous presentation of written and spoken words

Now we've learned that the simultaneous presentation of verbal and visual information can be beneficial, an easy mistake to make would be to start to present written words on the screen, and read them out for students at the same time. However, as we learned in relation to the redundancy effect, this is not a good idea for students who can already decode the language. How can this be? What's the difference between these two effects?

These effects are different in some subtle, but very important ways, and it can be easy to mix them up. To remedy this, the following summary table aims to clarify the key similarities and differences:

Similarity and difference table: redundancy and modality effects

	REDUNDANCY EFFECT Don't present written and spoken information in tandem	MODALITY EFFECT Do present images and spoken information in tandem
VISUAL INFORMATION PRESENTED	**Written text** Processed in **auditory** working memory	**Image** Processed in **visual** working memory
SPOKEN INFORMATION PRESENTED	**Spoken language** Processed in **auditory** working memory	
RESULT	The written and spoken information both compete for space in the same (auditory) channel, leading to redundancy and increased cognitive load	Presenting images and spoken language in tandem utilises the two channels of working memory and expands effective working memory capacity (reducing cognitive load)

Redundancy trap two: Simultaneous presentation of redundant information

It is hopefully now clear that the presentation of visual and spoken information in tandem can only be beneficial if the visual information is *not* written text. This is a necessary, but not a sufficient, condition for effective use of the modality effect. The second condition is that **dual-modality presentation can be effective so long as the verbal and visual information is unintelligible in isolation**. In the words of Sweller and colleagues:[116]

> *If the two sources of information can be understood in isolation, only one source, either the audio or the visual source should be used. If both are used, one source will be redundant and having to process both will lead to an extraneous cognitive load.*

This is the same as one of the key requirements to the split-attention effect. These similarities and differences are shown in the table below.

Similarity and difference table: split-attention and modality effects

	SPLIT-ATTENTION EFFECT Information that must be combined should be placed together in space and time	MODALITY EFFECT Utilise the visual and auditory channels of working memory in tandem
INFORMATION SOURCE 1	**Image** Processed in **visual** working memory	
INFORMATION SOURCE 2	**Written text** Processed in **auditory** working memory	**Spoken language** Processed in **auditory** working memory
MECHANISM	Placing the image and written text as close together as possible in space and time reduces the working memory load associated with information integration	Presenting images and spoken language in tandem utilises the two channels of working memory and expands effective working memory capacity (reducing cognitive load)
REQUIREMENT	Information source 1 and 2 must *only* be combined (split-attention) or simultaneously presented (modality) **if the two components are unintelligible in isolation**	

This idea of 'unintelligible in isolation' can be a bit hard to understand, so let's consider a simple example. In one study,[117] students received a verbal description

---

116. Sweller, J., Ayres, P. & Kalyuga, S. (2011) *Cognitive Load Theory.* Vol. 1. New York: Springer New York. p. 144.

117. Mayer, R.E. & Anderson, R.B. (1992) The instructive animation: Helping students build connections between words and pictures in multimedia learning. *Journal of Educational Psychology.* 84 (4), 444.

of how a bicycle pump works, along with animations of that same pump being operated. If students only received the verbal description without seeing the parts that were being referred to, this would not make sense. Alternatively, if they were just shown the animation of a pump without the description, they wouldn't have understood how it worked either. In this way, both the verbal description, and the animation, were each unintelligible in isolation, but together could facilitate understanding. In this context, combining them utilised the modality effect and enhanced learning.

> **Dual-modality presentation can be effective so long as the verbal and visual information is unintelligible in isolation.**

Modality and dual coding

A chapter on the modality effect would be incomplete without a mention of dual coding. The two are closely related, but are in fact quite distinct and often confused. In simple terms, the **modality effect relates to how information is presented**, whereas **dual coding relates to how information is remembered**.

The **modality effect** is concerned with **expanding effective working memory capacity *during* instruction**. In contrast, dual coding relates to the memory trace that remains in long-term memory after instruction. If that memory trace includes both word-based and image-based components that have been related to one another, then the key idea has been dual coded. Dual coding improves *memory stability*, because the information is stored in long-term memory in two different but connected ways. It also improves *retrievability*, because there are two separate environmental triggers for that memory to be retrieved, related words, or related images.[118]

> **The modality effect relates to cognitive load during instruction. Dual coding refers to the representation in long-term memory after instruction.**

The independence of dual coding theory and the modality effect becomes clearer when we consider the origins of Allan Paivio's original dual coding theory. Paivio's theory was first inspired by the 'one-bun, two-shoe' rhyming mnemonic technique. That is, the ancient knowledge that a list of items can

---

118. Paivio, A. (1990) *Mental representations: A dual coding approach* (Vol. 9). Abingdon: Oxford University Press. p. 69.

be more easily remembered if connected to a series of numbers; if we want to memorise the objects 'hamburger, shoes, stool' we can picture 'one hamburger, a *pair* of (two) shoes, a three-legged stool'. From this memorisation technique, Paivio hypothesised that the benefits of storing memories in both word-based and image-based forms were likely to extend beyond memorising mere lists of random items, to all memory encoding, which he called the *conceptual peg hypothesis*. It is from this hypothesis that dual coding theory was born.[119]

In this way, unlike the modality effect, Paivio's theory of dual coding does not rely in any way upon the model of working memory that proposes a visual and an auditory channel. In fact, working memory is referred to only twice in Paivio's 276-page book in which he outlines dual coding theory,[120] and never in relation to the theory itself. Put simply, **the modality effect relates to how information is presented, whereas dual coding relates to how information is remembered.**

> **The modality effect relates to how information is presented, whereas dual coding relates to how information is remembered.**

But the ideas of dual coding and the modality effect are related. Dual-modality presentation (as per the modality effect) can result in dual coding – the student may remember both the image and the verbal explanation given – but it isn't the only way that dual coding can occur. For example, a teacher could explain a concept entirely verbally, and a student could understand it well and lay down a long-term memory to represent that concept. At a later date, the student could encounter an image that represents the same idea, and could connect that image to the pre-existing concept stored in long-term memory. Now the words relating to the concept, and the image, are both stored and connected in long-term memory. From this point, related words or images within the environment could both act as a trigger for the memory of the concept. In this way, the memory has been dual coded, but the modality effect was never present.

In reality, the modality effect is an effective way to increase the likelihood of dual coding information. Importantly, it's a good way to do this while eliminating split-attention that could result from other attempted methods used to dual code information.

...

119. Paivio, A. (1991) Dual coding theory: Retrospect and current status. *Canadian Journal of Psychology/Revue canadienne de psychologie*. 45 (3), 255.
120. Paivio, A. (1990) *Mental representations: A dual coding approach* (Vol. 9). Abingdon: Oxford University Press. p. 69.

In closing this chapter on the modality effect, there's one final but important point to make. It's crucial that we don't think of the roughly four to seven elements of working memory capacity as simply 'divided' between visual and auditory memory components, nor does using both the auditory and visual components together enable us to 'double' our working memory capacity. Neither of these conceptions of working memory are true because the visual and auditory memory components are partly independent, and partly dependent. In terms of the modality effect, it's simply the case that using both channels for informational input allows us to present more information to students without overloading either of the single channels at a given time. In this way, 'the use of both channels increases the capacity of working memory'.[121]

> **The use of both auditory and visual channels in tandem increases the effective capacity of working memory.**

Department meeting idea

Now that we have covered several of the classic Cognitive Load Theory effects – redundancy, split-attention, transient information, and modality – you should be well placed to analyse some of your instructional resources in line with Cognitive Load Theory.

In a staff meeting or small group, take out a set of slides, a portion of a booklet, or some other teaching resource you'd like to analyse; just a sample, such as a few pages or slides, to start off with. Commence with a discussion about one or more of the redundancy, split-attention, transient information, or modality effects, using some of the examples within the preceding chapters as stimuli. If your group of teachers is quite familiar with these effects already, you may like to discuss all four. If the team is unfamiliar, starting with one is best.

Split your meeting into groups of two or three, and have each group take a copy of the same set of resources. Within a reasonable time-frame (for example, five minutes) have each group analyse the same set of resources with respect to the same effect, with a focus upon brainstorming how to best improve the resource in line with the effect. Have the groups compare their conclusions, and see if any groups have interpreted the implications of those effects differently to others, or seen opportunities to improve the

121. Sweller, J., Ayres, P. & Kalyuga, S. (2011) *Cognitive Load Theory*. Vol. 1. New York: Springer New York., p. 131.

resources in different ways to others. Be sure to also note things that are already done well within the resources, in line with Cognitive Load Theory.

If you are the department head, you may want to offer up your own resources for analysis first. This aligns with Dan Coyle's assertion that in order to build group trust, you can 'make sure the leader is vulnerable first and often'.[122] A leader offering up their own work for analysis signals an openness to improvement and models the belief that we can all get better as teachers, irrespective of our expertise or experience.

For a more advanced approach, split into four groups, one focused on each of the effects (redundancy, split-attention, transient information, modality), and collect four sets of *different* teaching resources, distributing one set to each group. Set a timer for five minutes, and have each group analyse their set of resources for their particular cognitive load effect. When the time is up, send the piles of resources clockwise to the next group, and analyse the next set. Continue for four rounds, until each set of resources has been analysed by each group, and in relation to each effect. Then come together at the end to discuss patterns in the resources, and ways they could be improved in line with these four Cognitive Load Theory recommendations.

---

122. Coyle, D. (2018) *The culture code: The secrets of highly successful groups.* London: Bantam.

Structure the practice

We have now surveyed a wide variety of strategies that enable us to effectively reduce extraneous load, and optimise intrinsic load, *during the presentation of information*. To add to this, we also require methods to *structure practice* and help students to make the transition from novice to expert in a given domain. This final section takes a detailed look at the recommendations that Cognitive Load Theory provides for achieving this goal.

Worked examples

In their seminal book on Cognitive Load Theory, Sweller, Ayres and Kalyuga write, 'Arguably, the worked example effect is the most important of the cognitive load theory effects.'[123] However, while the benefits of worked examples are perhaps the most famous and important of the cognitive load effects, they're also frequently misunderstood.

Most people familiar with the broad findings of Cognitive Load Theory are aware of the idea that worked example research usually compares learning via worked examples with learning via problem solving. Most are also aware that this research reports that, in the early stages of learning to complete a task, worked examples tend to be more efficient than solving problems as an instructional approach. The confusion arises, however, when we begin to explore what is meant by the terms, 'worked example', and 'problem solving'.

By way of example, consider the following experimental treatment, included in Sweller and Cooper's original study on the topic of worked examples:[124]

> *Firstly, present students with two well-structured worked examples, such as the following:*

1. For the equation $a = ag + b$, express a in terms of the other variables.

$$a = ag + b$$

$$a - ag = b$$

$$a(1 - g) = b$$

$$a = \frac{b}{1 - g}$$

---

123. Sweller, J., Ayres, P. & Kalyuga, S. (2011) Cognitive Load Theory. Vol. 1. New York: Springer New York. p. 108

124. Sweller, J. & Cooper, G.A. (1985) The use of worked examples as a substitute for problem solving in learning algebra. *Cognition and Instruction*. 2 (1), 59–89.

2. For the equation $\dfrac{b(a+c)}{e} = d$, express a in terms of the other variables.

$$\frac{b(a+c)}{e} = d$$

$$b(a+c) = ed$$

$$a + c = \frac{ed}{b}$$

$$a = \frac{ed}{b} - c$$

From Sweller and Cooper's original worked example study.[125]

Following this, ask them if they have any questions, and respond to students' questions until they report that they have a good understanding of the worked examples.

Finally, provide students with eight problems, four of each type, as practice.

Does this sound like teaching via worked examples to you?

It certainly did to me. Clear models are provided, students are given time to process them, ask questions to clarify, and then are given a set of similar examples to practice. It's also my guess that this treatment accurately reflects what most teachers would mean when they say, 'I teach using worked examples'.

The challenge is, however, that this isn't *at all* what Cognitive Load Theory means by 'worked examples'! In fact, the instructional procedure just described – present worked examples of two problem types, then give students practice on eight related problems – was the *problem solving* condition that Sweller and Cooper pitted against worked examples in this seminal study![126]

When I discovered this, I was shocked. I'd thought that *problem solving* within the Cognitive Load Theory research meant something like the National Council of Teachers of Mathematics' definition, 'engaging in a task for which the solution method is not known in advance'.[127] But this is not so; Cognitive

125. Sweller, J. & Cooper, G.A. (1985) The use of worked examples as a substitute for problem solving in learning algebra. *Cognition and Instruction*. 2 (1). p. 70.
126. Sweller, J. & Cooper, G.A. (1985) The use of worked examples as a substitute for problem solving in learning algebra. *Cognition and Instruction*. 2 (1), 59–89.
127. National Council of Teachers of Mathematics (NCTM) (2000) *Principles and standards for school mathematics*. Reston, VA: NCTM. p. 52, as cited in Foster, C. (2019) The fundamental problem with teaching problem solving. Available at: www.atm.org.uk

Load Theory's idea of problem solving was my idea of worked examples!

Within Cognitive Load Theory, the term 'worked examples' doesn't refer to the examples that are used to *teach* students how to solve a particular problem type in the first place. Instead, worked examples refer to the *guided practice* that students do following a teacher's initial exposition. In discussion with John Sweller, he described this as follows, 'The worked examples are a substitute for the lists of problems that students conventionally are asked to solve after the lesson. They are not a substitute for that lesson presented by the teacher.'[128]

> **Worked examples are a substitute for the lists of problems that students conventionally are asked to solve after the lesson. They are not a substitute for that lesson presented by the teacher. – *John Sweller***

In short, there is a phase of practice that sits between the teachers' instruction and students' fully independent practice that is best scaffolded with worked examples of increasing difficulty.

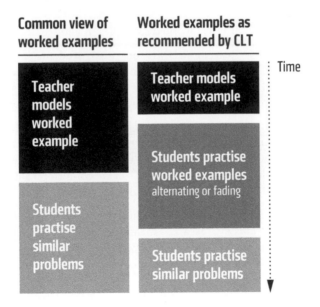

The remainder of this chapter focuses upon the effective design of worked examples that are intended for use in student practice.

---

128. Sweller, J. (2020) Personal communication, 17 June.

In reading the research, I have uncovered two core conditions for these types of worked examples to be successful. To make worked examples work, we must **structure** and **persist**.

By '**structure**' I mean that they must be constructed in such a way as to minimise extraneous load. This means taking into account the Cognitive Load Theory effects already outlined in this book, such as redundancy, transience, split-attention, and modality.

> *It is all too easy to assume that worked examples are effective because they are worked examples. A badly structured worked example presented to learners may be no more effective or even less effective than solving the equivalent problem. If extraneous cognitive load is not reduced compared to problem solving, the use of worked examples will not be effective.*[129]

By '**persist**' I mean that we must continue with worked examples for far longer than is traditionally seen as necessary. Sweller and colleagues write:

> *While worked examples are commonly employed until students are assumed to have obtained a basic familiarity with new material, the procedure is normally abandoned beyond this point to be replaced by conventional problems. It may be beneficial to persist with examples until complete familiarity with the material is attained.*[130]

We will now look at the two key methods for the delivery of worked examples found in the Cognitive Load Theory literature, **alternation** and **fading**.

The alternation strategy

'The most efficient method of studying examples and solving problems [is] to present a worked example and then immediately follow this example by asking the learner to solve a similar problem.'[131]

This is the alternation strategy, and it stands in contrast to the common practice of teachers spending the first 20-30 minutes of class modelling problems, then having students complete independent practice thereafter. In the conventional approach, students' working memories become completely overloaded during the long instructional phase, thus compromising learning, and they often become distracted or disinterested as a result.

129. Sweller, J., Ayres, P. & Kalyuga, S. (2011) *Cognitive Load Theory*. Vol. 1. New York: Springer New York. p. 107.

130. Sweller, J. & Cooper, G.A. (1985) The use of worked examples as a substitute for problem solving in learning algebra. *Cognition and Instruction*. 2 (1), 59–89. p. 87.

131. Sweller, J., Ayres, P. & Kalyuga, S. (2011) *Cognitive Load Theory*. Vol. 1. New York: Springer New York. p. 104.

By alternating between short, sharp worked examples, and similar problems for students to solve, the alternation strategy (also sometimes referred to as example-problem pairs) keeps instruction within the bounds of students' working memories.

The alternation strategy with worked examples

| worked example | similar problem | worked example | similar problem | worked example | similar problem | worked example | similar problem |

Time

Another clear benefit of the alternation strategy worth mentioning is its impact upon motivation, 'If learners expect a similar problem to be solved, they are motivated to process the example.'[132]

> The most efficient method of studying examples and solving problems [is] to present a worked example and then immediately follow this example by asking the learner to solve a similar problem. – *John Sweller*

The alternation strategy in mathematics

In mathematics, a sequence of two example-problem pairs could look as follows:

Worked example 1.	Similar problem 1.
Question: Solve $3x - 6 = 12$ for x	Question: Solve $2x - 4 = 10$ for x
Step 1: Add 6 to both sides then simplify	
$3x - 6 + 6 = 12 + 6$	
$3x = 18$	
Step 2: Divide both sides by 3 then simplify	
$\dfrac{3x}{3} = \dfrac{18}{3}$	
$x = 6$	

---

132. Renkl, A. (2014) Toward an instructionally oriented theory of example-based learning. *Cognitive Science.* 38 (1), 1–37. p. 4.

Worked example 2.	Similar problem 2.
Question: Solve $3x + 6 = 12$ for x Step 1: Subtract 6 from both sides then simplify $$3x + 6 - 6 = 12 - 6$$ $$3x = 6$$ Step 2: Divide both sides by 3 then simplify $$\frac{\cancel{3}x}{\cancel{3}} = \frac{6}{3}$$ $$x = 2$$	Question: Solve $2x + 4 = 10$ for x

This is a base-level sequence of two example-problem pairs (we'll build upon this in the following chapter on self-explanation), but from it we can already see some key features. Firstly, there's minimal difference between the worked example, and the matched problem for students to solve. Secondly, there is only one simple variation between worked example 1 and worked example 2 (a subtraction changed to an addition).

By ensuring only a small amount of variation between example and problem, and between sequential worked examples, we can keep a tight handle on the cognitive load that students are experiencing. This sequence may seem 'too simple' for some students, and it will be, but if students are truly algebra novices, this 'little variation' approach is likely to help them progress through the content at an appropriate rate.

The alternation strategy in science

Distinguishing between independent and dependent variables is a task that students often struggle with. Example-problem pairs to assist students in making this distinction could look as follows:

Worked example 1.	Similar problem 1.
Students conducted an experiment in which they dropped a ball from different heights and timed how long it took to hit the ground.	A teacher ran an experiment in which they changed the concentration of salt in a solution and measured the specific heat capacity of the solution.
Question: Indentify the independent and dependent variables in this experiment and justify your choice.	Question: Identify the independent and dependent variables in this experiment and justify your choice.
The independent variable is drop height (metres). This is because drop height is the variable that was altered by the experimenters. The dependent variable is fall time (seconds). This is as the fall time is what was impacted by changing the independent variable.	

Worked example 1.	Similar problem 1.
A group of students recorded changes in the period of a pendulum (how long it took to swing back and forth) that were generated by varying its mass.	A scientist recorded how the range (how far the projectile travelled) of a catapult changed based upon variations in its initial launch angle.
Question: Indentify the independent and dependent variables in this experiment and justify your choice.	Question: Identify the independent and dependent variables in this experiment and justify your choice.
The independent variable is pendulum mass (kg). This is because mass is the variable that was altered by the experimenters. The dependent variable is period (seconds). This is as period is what was impacted by changing the independent variable.	

As with the mathematics example, here we also have only a small amount of variation between worked examples 1 and 2. The main change in this sequence is the order in which the independent and dependent variables have been mentioned in the initial description of the experiment.

This activity would also be aided by pre-teaching of the key vocabulary likely to be used in such a scenario, including words and phrases representing variation (vary, change, alter, manipulate) and causality (based upon, because of, generated by, as a result of).

The alternation strategy in English

For students to eloquently express their ideas, they must have a firm understanding of the appropriate use of a broad array of sentence structures. Here's an example of how worked examples can support students to learn to appropriately employ crucial sentence 'templates' to express their ideas.

Worked examples.	Similar problem 1.
We are practising using the phrase	Write a sentence using '... . *In contrast, ...*' for each of the topics below.
'... In contrast, ...'	
'In contrast' is used to show that the ideas presented before and after the 'in contrast' are opposites, or almost opposites.	*Don't forget this comma!*
Food example:	Food example:
My favourite food is baked beans. **In contrast,** my brother hates them!	
Film example:	Film example:
Harry thinks that *The Matrix* is an excellent film. **In contrast,** I think it's boring.	
Sport example:	Sport example:
I am very bad at soccer. **In contrast,** Faduma is amazing!	
Music example:	Music example:
My Dad loves classical music. **In contrast,** My mum is a big fan of heavy metal.	
Example from school subjects (harder):	Example from school subjects (harder):
In English we indicate that we are asking a question by raising the pitch of our voice at the end of a sentence. In contrast, in Mandarin a question is indicated by saying 'ma' at the end of a sentence.	

This approach can be used for all manner of sentence structures, new vocabulary, or the writing of longer form pieces. For English teachers keen to explore further the effective use of example-problem pairs (and much more) I highly recommend *The Writing Revolution* by Judith Hochman and Natalie Wexler, as well as Tom Needhan's collection of blog posts on *Applying Cognitive Load Theory to English.*[133]

Worked examples can also be used to teach full essays. In one study,[134] a group of English literature students were provided with worked examples in the form of model essays. These were on similar, but not identical, topics to those on which the students subsequently wrote. It was found that students who studied the worked examples produced better final essays than a control group. This occurred even though the control group was given extra essay writing practice to match the study time of the worked example group.

---

133. These posts can be found at http://tiny.cc/tomneedhamclt
134. Kyun, S., Kalyuga, S. & Sweller, J. (2013) The effect of worked examples when learning to write essays in English literature. *The Journal of Experimental Education*. 81 (3), 385–408.

I experienced a similar benefit of worked examples when I was writing my Master's thesis. I felt totally lost and didn't know where to start until I tracked down two examples of high quality Master's theses on slightly related topics. Suddenly I had clarity around what I was trying to produce. Models of writing aid students in understanding what is expected of them, and allow them to see the kinds of structures and approaches that expert writers employ to communicate their ideas.

The alternation strategy with homework

As a teacher often faced with students who hand in unfinished homework because they 'got stuck', one of the most exciting arenas of worked example research examines their efficacy when used during homework. A study by Ward and Sweller[135] had a control group of students complete ten standard homework problems (five pairs of very similar problems), compared to an alternating worked example condition, as pictured.

Task	1a	1b	2a	2b	3a	3b	4a	4b	5a	5b
Control	Problem	Problem	Problem	Problem	Problem	Problem	Problem	Problem	Problem	Problem
Worked Example Group	Worked Example	Problem	Worked Example	Problem	Worked Example	Problem	Worked Example	Problem	Worked Example	Problem

Students in the worked example group performed significantly better on a test the following day, despite the fact they had only answered five instead of ten problems themselves. We usually think of homework as 'consolidation' time, but it's often the case that students aren't yet ready to consolidate, they're still firmly in the acquisition phase of learning. Again, we're reminded that, 'It may be beneficial to persist with examples until complete familiarity with the material is attained.'[136] **Persist!**

The alternation strategy with student reflections

Worked examples have also proved useful in supporting students to improve the quality of their reflective learning journals. Hübner and colleagues demonstrated that through exposure to worked examples, students learned to more effectively reflect on their learning; an effect which translated to both

---

135. Ward, M. & Sweller, J. (1990) Structuring effective worked examples. *Cognition and Instruction*. 7 (1), 1–39.

136. Sweller, J. & Cooper, G.A. (1985) The use of worked examples as a substitute for problem solving in learning algebra. *Cognition and Instruction*. 2 (1), 59–89. p. 87.

better journaling in the next learning topic, and to improved learning outcomes in the next topic (both examples of transfer).[137]

Faded worked examples

In situations where the jump from a fully worked example to an independently completed similar problem may be too challenging for students, fading can be a powerful strategy to use. **Fading** – also referred to as 'completion problems' – refers to the process of presenting students first with a complete worked example, and next with a similar worked example with only one line of working missing. Lines are progressively omitted until students are completing full problems independently, as shown in the diagram below.[138]

Faded worked examples, overview

The process pictured above is referred to as 'backward fading' as the first line omitted is the final line of the worked example. 'Forward fading' occurs when the first missing line for students to complete is the first line of the worked example. I have also experimented with what I have called 'contour fading', which commences the fading process first with the most difficult line within the worked example (the 'peak'), and fades evenly in the forwards and backwards directions from that critical solution point.

Schwonke, Renkl and colleagues found that fading worked examples led to faster learning time and deeper conceptual understanding, even when compared to a

---

137. Hübner, S., Nückles, M. & Renkl, A. (2010) Writing learning journals: Instructional support to overcome learning-strategy deficits. *Learning and Instruction*, 20, 18–29. https://doi.org/10.1016/j.learninstruc.2008.12.001.
138. Inspired by Clark, R.C., Nguyen, F. & Sweller, J. (2011) *Efficiency in learning: Evidence-based guidelines to manage cognitive load.* New Jersey: Wiley. p. 199.

highly scaffolded computer-based learning environment in which 'At any point in time, the student [could] request a hint from the tutor' and where students received, 'appropriate just-in-time feedback and hints on basis of a computational model'.[139]

Faded worked examples in English

The previously presented alternation problems for English could be turned into faded problems in the following manner, which could be helpful for primary school students, EAL students, or high school students who are particularly struggling.

Faded worked examples.	Practice 3b:
We are practising using the phrase,	My best friend isn't very good at table tennis. **In** contrast _____.
'.... In contrast, ...'	Practice 3c:
'In contrast' is used to show that the ideas presented before and after the 'In contrast' are opposites, or almost opposites.	I really like to listen to rap. **In contrast** _____ _____.
Example:	Practice 4a:
My favourite food is baked beans. **In contrast**, my brother hates them!	My teacher likes to eat curry. _____ _____.
Practice 1a:	Practice 4b:
Harry thinks that *The Matrix* is an excellent film. **In contrast**, I think it's _____.	My teacher is a big fan of tennis. _____ _____.
Practice 1b:	Practice 4c:
I am very bad at soccer. **In contrast**, Faduma is _____!	My grandma likes to listen to jazz music. _____ _____.
Practice 1c:	5a. Create your own food example:
My Dad loves classical music. **In contrast**, my mum is a big fan of _____.	
Practice 2a:	5b. Create your own sport example:
My favourite food is baked beans. **In contrast**, _____ _____.	
Practice 2b:	5c. Create your own music example:
My best friend isn't very good at table tennis. **In** contrast, _____.	
Practice 2c:	6. Create an example of your choice:
I really like to listen to rap. **In contrast**, _____ _____.	
For parts 3, 4, and 5 remember to add this comma after the 'In contrast'.	
Practice 3a:	
My favourite food is baked beans. **In contrast** _____	

139. Schwonke, R., Renkl, A., Krieg, C., Wittwer, J., Aleven, V. & Salden, R. (*2009*) The worked-example effect: Not an artefact of lousy control conditions. *Computers in Human Behavior* 25 (2009) 258–266 p. 260.

As you can see, each of the phases 1, 2, 3, 4, and 5 gives students the opportunity to practice more and more of the exercise themselves. It is also worth noting that while the examples above are all presented together, it would be useful for students to complete this sequence over several lessons, beneficially spacing their practice.

Faded worked examples in music

If a student is struggling with a particularly difficult set of bars in a challenging piece, fading can be usefully employed here too. Students can be encouraged to play the final bar, or even the final combination of notes at first, and progressively work backwards as they master the piece.[140]

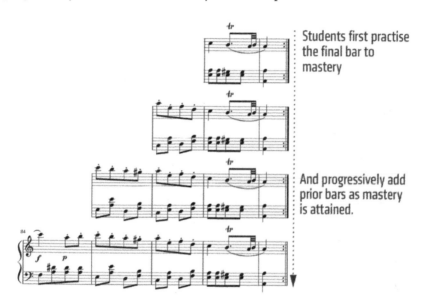

Students first practise the final bar to mastery

And progressively add prior bars as mastery is attained.

This approach has an added benefit in that it ensures a strong finish for students and prepares them to 'pick up' playing a piece from multiple different positions. This avoids the issue that sometimes occurs whereby, when a student makes a mistake, they find that they need to go back to the beginning of the section and start again before they are able to continue.

Paul Owen's PhD focused on the application of Cognitive Load Theory to music instruction. Within Owen's work, it was demonstrated that worked examples are also highly effective when applied to the domain of music theory.[141]

---

140. The full score is available at: http://tiny.cc/rondoallaturca-source
141. Owens, P. & Sweller, J. (2008) Cognitive load theory and music instruction. *Educational Psychology.* 28 (1), 29–45.

Faded worked examples in lower primary

When students are learning to count, or learning to recite the alphabet, they often find that if they make a mistake, they have to start all over again from the beginning. 'Counting on' is an invaluable skill for students to master in the early stages of numeracy.

For example, when adding seven plus three, many students will first count up to seven, and only after first counting to seven will then continue with, 'eight, nine, ten'. Backwards fading with counting can help students to learn to 'count on' at a faster rate than they may develop otherwise.

This could initially begin as illustrated below:

> *Teacher: Today, instead of us all counting to ten together, I'm going to count to nine, then I want you to say 'ten' when it's time. Here goes. One, two, three, four, five, six, seven, eight, nine...*
>
> *Students: 'Ten'*
>
> *Teacher: Good. Let's practice a few more times.*
>
> *(Does so)*
>
> *Teacher: Ok, now I'm going to count to eight and I want you to then say, 'nine, ten'. Here goes...*

This is a powerful approach to supporting students to 'count on'. Once students can do this, the teacher can progressively eliminate the numbers from the start of the count. That could look like this:

> *Teacher: We're going to do the same thing now, but I'm not going to start with 'one'. Instead I'm going to start with 'two'. After I say 'nine', you just have to say 'ten'.*
>
> *(Does so, can clap or tap to mark the 'one')*
>
> *Teacher: This time I'm going to start at 'three', and when I get to 'eight', you say after me 'nine, ten'.*

Eventually, the class will get to the point that they can conduct oral counting activities such as this:

> *Teacher: Start after seven, count on three more.*
>
> *Students: Eight, nine, ten.*

Teacher: Start after four, count on four more.

Students: Five, six, seven, eight.

A similar approach can be used to help students to navigate the alphabet without needing to go back to the start each time.

A fading approach can also be used to support students to skip count. If the teacher plans to help students to learn to skip count by threes,[142] the progression could proceed as follows:

- Students count out loud together to 36.

- Count to 36 emphasising (loudly, it's fun!) every third number.

- Count to 36 whispering the numbers in between every third number.

- Count to 36 emphasising every third number and whispering all other numbers.

- Count to 36 only saying every third number but tapping along on desks for other numbers.

- Do the same, but this time without overtly tapping.

- Do the same, challenge students not to bob their heads or do anything that can externally be seen as counting.

- Skip count from 0 to 36 by threes.

Depending upon the students, this may be achievable in a single lesson, or may be better achieved over several lessons. Ensure that you reinforce this ability by regularly returning to the skill until students have automatised it.

Why do worked examples work?

As we now know, a key difference between experts and novices within a given domain is the collection of situation → action pairs that they have stored in long-term memory. Experts have a vast and well-organised collection, and their use of these pairs in relevant situations is automatic. This is in contrast to novices, who have only a limited collection of these situation → action pairs, each of which is slow and effortful to call upon, and is sometimes utilised at an inappropriate time.

This means that, in order for us to help novices to become experts, we first need to help them build their collection of situation → action pairs, and to

---

142. Example inspired by a Ron Yoshimoto workshop at *INVESTed Sharing Best Practice* conference. Gippsland, Victoria, 2020.

organise this collection in long-term memory in an appropriate way. Organised collections of such pairs – or any knowledge for that matter – are collectively referred to as 'schemas'.[143]

Given this, the question becomes, 'What is the quickest and most efficient way to help students to build this collection of situation → action pairs?' To this question, Cognitive Load Theory suggests that the quickest way to get any well-organised knowledge into long-term memory is to borrow it from an expert, the so-called 'borrowing and reorganising principle';[144] and worked examples facilitate this. Put simply, worked examples 'provide an expert's problem-solving model for the learner to study and emulate'.[145]

> **The quickest way to get *any* well-organised knowledge into long-term memory is to borrow it from an expert.**

This approach is efficient because it minimises the chance that what students learn will be incorrect. When students discover connections for themselves, there's a good chance that these connections may not be accurate. This is not so for knowledge structures borrowed from an expert. In the words of Sweller *et al*, 'Borrowed information has already been organised and is likely to be appropriate ... because it has already been tested for effectiveness.'[146] The value of borrowing well organised information from an expert becomes clear when we consider the number of 'misconceptions' that students naturally hold. Misconceptions are incorrect knowledge schemas that students have built based upon their own reasoning about the world. Through schema borrowing from experts, the number of misconceptions that novices hold, and are likely to form, can be reduced.

This is how worked examples work. They're an efficient way to help novices to acquire the knowledge structures of experts.

---

143. Chi, M., Glaser, R. & Rees, E. (1982) Expertise in problem solving. In R. Sternberg (Ed.), *Advances in the psychology of human intelligence* (pp. 7–75). Hillsdale: Lawrence Erlbaum, as cited in Sweller, J., Ayres, P. & Kalyuga, S. (2011) *Cognitive Load Theory*. Vol. 1. New York: Springer New York. pp. 22-23.

144. Sweller, J., Ayres, P. & Kalyuga, S. (2011) *Cognitive Load Theory*. Vol. 1. New York: Springer New York.

145. Atkinson, R.K., Derry, S.J., Renkl, A. & Wortham, D. (2000) Learning from examples: Instructional principles from the worked examples research. *Review of Educational Research*, 70(2), 181-214. p. 181.

146. Sweller, J., Ayres, P. & Kalyuga, S. (2011) *Cognitive Load Theory*. Vol. 1. New York: Springer New York. p. 31.

Boundary conditions for the worked example effect

As with all the cognitive load effects mentioned previously, the expertise reversal effect becomes relevant as students move beyond the novice phase during learning. Once students have the knowledge required to solve a particular problem type, they will benefit more from problem solving practice than further worked examples. This is because problem solving provides intermediate students with the practice they need to take the next step towards expertise, automation.[147]

...

This chapter has dealt with the role of the teacher in providing worked examples of the right structure, at an appropriate level of difficulty, in a suitable fashion, and for the correct duration; **structure, fade, alternate, persist**. However, the student also has a crucial role to play in making best use of the learning opportunities that worked examples provide, and this is the topic of the next chapter.

Self-explanation

In order for students to get the most out of a worked example, it is not sufficient for them to simply use the example as a model to solve similar problems, they must also self-explain it.[148] **Students are self-explaining when they explain an example to themselves in terms of its underlying principles, or when they explain to themselves why a particular principle can be applied to a specific example.**[149] While this definition, and this chapter, focuses on self-explaining while studying worked examples, students can also engage in self-explanation while solving problems or while reading texts. This chapter also focuses on principle-based self-explanation, which is only a subset of self-explanation as it is broadly defined within the literature.

> **Students are self-explaining when they explain an example to themselves in terms of its underlying principles, or when they explain to themselves why a particular principle can be applied to a specific example.**

Principle-based self-explanations are particularly important for two main reasons. Firstly, connecting examples to their underlying principles allows

---

147. Kalyuga, S., Chandler, P., Tuovinen, J. & Sweller, J. (2001) When problem solving is superior to studying worked examples. *Journal of Educational Psychology*, 93, 579–588.
148. Busch, C., Renkl, A. & Schworm, S. (2008) Towards a generic self-explanation training intervention for example-based learning.
149. Renkl, A. & Eitel, A. (2019) Self-explaining: learning about principles and their application. In J. Dunlosky & K. Rawson (Eds.), *Cambridge Handbook of Cognition and Education*, 528–549.

students to see past the surface features of a problem to the deep structure.[150] Experts categorise problems by their underlying structure, whereas novices classify them by their surface features,[151] so supporting students to focus upon deep structure helps them to build their knowledge in a way that reflects that of an expert. Secondly, a principle-based approach provides a basis for transfer to new problems. Through this 'analogical reasoning',[152] when faced with a similar example in the future, students can think to themselves, 'This looks like that problem that I saw before, maybe I can apply a similar principle here!'

The primary method for helping students to begin to self-explain effectively is to *prompt* them to do so. But not all self-explanation prompts are created equal. A core characteristic of self-explanation prompts is where they sit on the spectrum from example-specific to general. **Example-specific self-explanation prompts** are inserted into worked examples at specific times to prompt students' self-explanations there and then. **General self-explanation prompts** are designed to support students to develop the habit of self-explanation, with the aim of these habits transferring to new situations in future.

This specific-to-general spectrum also applies to educational instruction more generally. The spectrum is important because contained within it is a set of trade-offs. More specific and concrete instructional approaches deliver quicker and more reliable results, but those results are unlikely to transfer to situations that aren't immediately similar. In contrast, more general and abstract approaches leave in-the-moment learning success much more to chance, but when learning does occur, that learning is more likely to transfer to new and different situations. This is also the case for example-specific versus general self-explanation prompts. This important idea of specific versus general benefits and trade-offs will become clearer through consideration of the following examples.

Example-specific self-explanation prompts

The following examples demonstrate a series of example-specific self-explanation prompts from a variety of subjects. They also move from more

150. Chi, M.T. & Van Lehn, K.A. (2012) Seeing deep structure from the interactions of surface features. *Educational Psychologist*, 47(3), 177-188.

151. Chi, M.T., Feltovich, P.J. & Glaser, R. (1981) Categorization and representation of physics problems by experts and novices. *Cognitive Science*, 5(2), 121-152.

152. Ross, B.H. (1989) Reminders in learning and instruction. In S. Vosniadou & A. Ortony (Eds.), *Similarity and analogical reasoning* (pp. 438–469). Cambridge: Cambridge. University Press. As cited in Renkl. R & Eitel. R (2019) Self Explaining: Learning about Principles and Their Application, pp. 528-549 in Dunlosky, J. & Rawson, K.A. (Eds.). (2019) *The Cambridge Handbook of Cognition and Education. Cambridge*: Cambridge University Press.

highly scaffolded, such as multiple choice prompts, to less scaffolded, such as free-response prompts.

Example-specific self-explanation prompts in mathematics

In the previous chapter we looked at a worked example demonstrating the process of solving $3x - 6 = 12$ for x. The issue with this worked example was that, while it showed all the necessary steps, there was no reference to *why* each step was made, or *how* a student would know which action to take in each line of working. That is, it was devoid of any discussion of principles.

To improve upon this, students must be supported to link the initial example to principles that can be used to solve it, and other similar questions in future. For equations like these, one effective approach is to teach 'SMEG'. SMEG stands for: subtraction (and addition), multiplication (and division), exponents, groups.[153]

To have students self-explain this principle, they first must be taught it. This would need to be done over a significant period of time, but one such worked example within that time period could look as follows:

Worked example 1.	Similar problem 1.
Question: Solve $3x - 6 = 12$ for x	Question: Solve $2x - 4 = 10$ for x
Ask: In order to solve for x what do we need to eliminate?	
Answer: The operations on the x's side, which are ×3 and −6	
Ask: Which of these do we try to eliminate first?	
Answer: 'S' (subtraction and addition) is first in SMEG, so we eliminate the −6 first using its inverse operation, + 6	
Step 1: Add 6 to both sides then simplify	
$$3x - 6 + 6 = 12 + 6$$	
$$3x = 18$$	
Ask: What is your next step?	
Answer: We can now eliminate the remaining ×3 using its inverse operation ÷ 3	
Step 2: Divide both sides by 3 then simplify	
$$\frac{\cancel{3}x}{\cancel{3}} = \frac{18}{3}$$	
$$x = 6$$	

---

153. The SMEG-based worked example and self-explanation problem in this section is inspired by a blog post by Dani Quinn. Available at: https://missquinnmaths.wordpress.com/2018/11/23/tried-and-tested-solving-with-smeg/

Once students are somewhat familiar with the SMEG approach, they could transition to self-explanation questions, such as the following (note: the handwriting in the following example represents an ideal response from a student. You would not provide the self-explanation activity to students with answers filled in):

Worked example.	Self-explanation prompts.
Dani completed the question below as follows:	**Q:** In step 1, how did Dani know to start by eliminating the $+6$ instead of the $\times 3$?
Question: Solve $3x + 6 = 12$ for x	
Step 1: Subtract 6 from both sides then simplify	*Dani knew that to get the **x** by itself, she needed to eliminate the **×3** and the **+6**. Dani thought of 'SMEG' and realised that she should eliminate the subtraction (SMEG) first.*
$3x + 6 - 6 = 12 - 6$	
$3x = 6$	
Step 2: Divide both sides by 3 then simplify	**Q:** In step 2, how did Dani know to divide both sides by 3?
$\dfrac{3x}{3} = \dfrac{6}{3}$	*Dani wanted to eliminate the **×3**, so she knew to use its inverse operation, ÷3.*
$x = 2$	

The sample student response provided above is the level of understanding of principles that we want to support in all students.

It is important to emphasise here that such self-explanation prompts need not require a written response. Another very effective approach could be to show a worked example on the board along with these self-explanation prompts, have students pair share their answers, then cold call (pick at random, often using pop-sticks) a student to share. In fact, oral practice of such self-explanations is the perfect bridge to written responses.

If students aren't yet ready to self-explain in full sentences, another way they can be scaffolded to do so is with fill-in-the-blank self-explanation prompts, referred to as 'assisting' self-explanation prompts in the literature.[154] Here's an example:

---

154. Berthold, K., Eysink, T.H. & Renkl, A. (2009) Assisting self-explanation prompts are more effective than open prompts when learning with multiple representations. *Instructional Science*, 37(4), 345-363. p. 346.

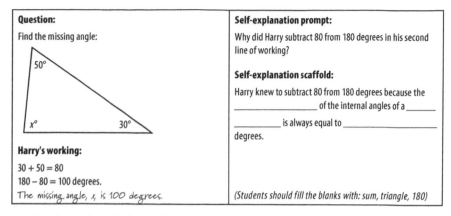

Question:	Self-explanation prompt:
Find the missing angle:	Why did Harry subtract 80 from 180 degrees in his second line of working?
50° ... x° ... 30°	**Self-explanation scaffold:**
	Harry knew to subtract 80 from 180 degrees because the _____ of the internal angles of a _____
Harry's working:	_____ is always equal to _____ degrees.
30 + 50 = 80	
180 − 80 = 100 degrees.	
The missing angle, x, is 100 degrees.	*(Students should fill the blanks with: sum, triangle, 180)*

Studies have found that self-explanation prompts accompanied by fill-in-the-blank scaffolds lead to greater learning *for novices* than simply the prompt in isolation and without the scaffold.[155]

In more demanding scenarios, there may be a range of principles, rules, or laws that students often confuse. As such, the first challenge they face is selecting which rule is appropriate for a given problem. In these situations, it can be helpful for self-explanation prompts to directly target this initial decision. Here is part of a sequence of rapid-fire questions of this type that I used to help one of my senior mathematics classes to identify when to use the chain, product, or quotient rule to differentiate. I created this using the freely available software Desmos[156] (each of the six questions pictured below was presented on successive slides).

155. Berthold, K., Eysink, T.H. & Renkl, A. (2009) Assisting self-explanation prompts are more effective than open prompts when learning with multiple representations. *Instructional Science*, 37(4), 345-363. p. 346 and Berthold, K. & Renkl, A. (2009) Instructional aids to support a conceptual understanding of multiple representations. *Journal of Educational Psychology*, 101(1), 70.

156. More information on Desmos can be found at: https://teacher.desmos.com/

Which rule should you use?	Which rule should you use?	Which rule should you use?
Find $\frac{d}{dx}\sqrt{2x+3}$	Find $\frac{d}{dx}\frac{3x^2}{\sin(x)}$	Find $\frac{d}{dx}3(4x)^2$
(don't actually find it, just select which of the three rules you would need to use for this question)	(don't actually find it, just select which of the three rules you would need to use for this question)	(don't actually find it, just select which of the three rules you would need to use for this question)
○ It looks like $\frac{d}{dx}u(v(x))$ so I should use the chain rule.	○ It looks like $\frac{d}{dx}u(v(x))$ so I should use the chain rule.	○ It looks like $\frac{d}{dx}u(v(x))$ so I should use the chain rule.
○ It looks like $\frac{d}{dx}u(x)v(x)$ so I should use the product rule.	○ It looks like $\frac{d}{dx}u(x)v(x)$ so I should use the product rule.	○ It looks like $\frac{d}{dx}u(x)v(x)$ so I should use the product rule.
○ It looks like $\frac{d}{dx}\frac{u(x)}{v(x)}$ so I should use the quotient rule.	○ It looks like $\frac{d}{dx}\frac{u(x)}{v(x)}$ so I should use the quotient rule.	○ It looks like $\frac{d}{dx}\frac{u(x)}{v(x)}$ so I should use the quotient rule.
Screen 1	*Screen 2*	*Screen 3*
Which rule should you use?	Which rule should you use?	Which rule should you use?
Find $\frac{d}{dx}\ln(4x)\cdot 5x^2$	Find $\frac{d}{dx}e^x\sin(x)$	Find $\frac{d}{dx}\frac{45x^2}{\ln(x+2)}$
(don't actually find it, just select which of the three rules you would need to use for this question)	(don't actually find it, just select which of the three rules you would need to use for this question)	(don't actually find it, just select which of the three rules you would need to use for this question)
○ It looks like $\frac{d}{dx}u(v(x))$ so I should use the chain rule.	○ It looks like $\frac{d}{dx}u(v(x))$ so I should use the chain rule.	○ It looks like $\frac{d}{dx}u(v(x))$ so I should use the chain rule.
○ It looks like $\frac{d}{dx}u(x)v(x)$ so I should use the product rule.	○ It looks like $\frac{d}{dx}u(x)v(x)$ so I should use the product rule.	○ It looks like $\frac{d}{dx}u(x)v(x)$ so I should use the product rule.
○ It looks like $\frac{d}{dx}\frac{u(x)}{v(x)}$ so I should use the quotient rule.	○ It looks like $\frac{d}{dx}\frac{u(x)}{v(x)}$ so I should use the quotient rule.	○ It looks like $\frac{d}{dx}\frac{u(x)}{v(x)}$ so I should use the quotient rule.
Screen 4	*Screen 5*	*Screen 6*

Opposite is another example of multiple-choice self-explanation prompts, this time from a study on effective self-explanation prompts in teaching probability in a computer-assisted environment[157]

---

157. Atkinson, R.K., Renkl, A. & Merrill, M.M. (2003) Transitioning from studying examples to solving problems: Effects of self-explanation prompts and fading worked-out steps. *Journal of Educational Psychology.* 95 (4), 774.

Problem Text

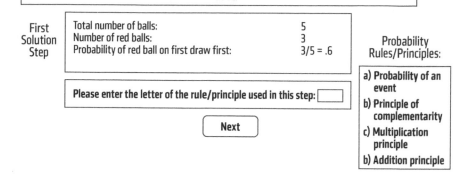

Example-specific self-explanation in chemistry

As well as these highly scaffolded approaches, a less scaffolded, simple prompt can sometimes be better than none at all. Crippen and Earl provide an example of this as applied to chemistry.[158] Students were provided with the following worked example:

Worked examples

Iron is oxidised and nickel is reduced in the example reaction below

Balanced Chemical	$Fe_{(s)}$	$Ni(NO_3)_{2(aq)}$	$Fe(NO_3)_{2(aq)}$	$Ni_{(s)}$
Oxidation States	(0)	$(+2)[(+5)(-2)3]2$	$(+2)[(+5)(-2)3]2$	(0)
Action	Oxidised	Reduced		
Function	Reducing Agent	Oxidising Agent		

---

158. Crippen, K.J. & Earl, B.L. (2007) The impact of web-based worked examples and self-explanation on performance, problem solving, and self-efficacy. *Computers & Education*, 49(3), 809-821 p. 815.

Then some participants were provided with the following prompt, and some were not.

> *A **suggestion:** After studying the example, explain to yourself how the terms oxidised, reduced, oxidising agent, and reducing agent are used. Consider both their relation to each other as words and phrases, as well as to chemical compounds in a balanced chemical equation.*[159]

Those provided with this self-explanation prompt, encouraging them to interrogate their understanding of the key terms within the example, did significantly better than those not presented with the prompt.

Example-specific self-explanation in foreign language learning

If learning German, a student could be presented with a question such as the following:

Worked example.	Self-explanation prompts.
Faiza was practising the use of *habe, hast, hat, haben,* and *habt* in German. She answered a question as follows.	Question: How did Faiza know to use 'hast' in the first sentence?
Complete the sentence:	
Sentence 1: *Was* _hast_ *du gesagt?*	Question: How did Faiza know to use 'habe' in the second sentence?
Sentence 2: *Ich* _habe_ *dich nicht verstanden.*	

If students are simply asked to answer a set of grammar questions such as those above, they could do so without spending any time considering *why* they're giving each answer in each case. Inserting this self-explanation prompt encourages them to link the answers back to the principles of German grammar the teacher is trying to reinforce. Asking students to explain the answer also gives the teacher a clearer insight into the strength of their understanding of these key German grammar principles, rather than trying to infer their grammar understanding from answers alone.

Self-explanation of incorrect answers

Another approach to self-explanation is to have students self-explain incorrect answers. However, if you do try this, it's important to keep the following in mind. Firstly, students *must* be aware that they're explaining an *incorrect* example. Students self-explaining incorrect examples as if they are correct serves to only

---

159. Crippen, K.J. & Earl, B.L. (2007) The impact of web-based worked examples and self-explanation on performance, problem solving, and self-efficacy. *Computers & Education,* 49(3), 809-821 p. 815.

encode the incorrect procedure into memory.[160] This is a particularly important point to keep in mind when students are encouraged to explain their own thinking. Rittle-Johnson *et al* write, 'Prompting children to explain their own predictions, which were often incorrect, reduced their subsequent success at making evidence-based claims relative to a no-explanation condition.'[161]

Prompting students to compare and contrast *correct* and *incorrect* worked examples can be effective too.[162] If taking this approach, it's important to consider that: 1. This approach introduces more interacting elements, so may help stronger learners, but overwhelm students with insufficient prior knowledge.[163] 2. If students are asked to explain correct and incorrect examples, it is helpful to present both side-by-side in order to increase the chances that they notice the differences.[164]

160. Berthold, K. & Renkl, A. (2009) Instructional aids to support a conceptual understanding of multiple representations. *Journal of Educational Psychology.* 101 (1), p. 70.

161. Rittle-Johnson, B. & Loehr, A.M. (2017) Eliciting explanations: Constraints on when self-explanation aids learning. *Psychonomic Bulletin & Review.* 24 (5), pp.1501–1510.

162. Rittle-Johnson, B., Loehr, A.M. & Durkin, K. (2017) Promoting self-explanation to improve mathematics learning: A meta-analysis and instructional design principles. *ZDM.* 49 (4), pp. 599–611.

163. Große, C.S. & Renkl, A. (2007) Finding and fixing errors in worked examples: Can this foster learning outcomes? *Learning and instruction,* 17(6), pp. 612-634

164. Renkl. R & Eitel. R (2019) Self Explaining: Learning about Principles and Their Application, pp. 528-549 in Dunlosky, J. & Rawson, K.A. (Eds.) (2019) *The Cambridge Handbook of Cognition and Education.* Cambridge: Cambridge University Press.

Here's an example of such a 'compare and contrast' approach which was used in teacher education training:[165]

The Building Blocks Principle II

A tiler needed 720 tiles for an area of 16 m² in the bathroom. He wants to use the same tiles for an area of 2.4 m² in the kitchen.
How many tiles does he need in the kitchen?

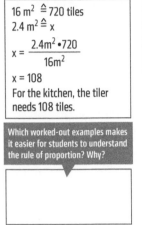

$$16 \, m^2 \triangleq 720 \text{ tiles}$$
$$2.4 \, m^2 \triangleq x$$
$$x = \frac{2.4 m^2 \cdot 720}{16 m^2}$$
$$x = 108$$

For the kitchen, the tiler needs 108 tiles.

16 m² = 720 tiles   :16
:16
1 m² = 45 tiles
•2.4   •2.4
2.4 m² = 108 tiles

For the kitchen, the tiler needs 108 tiles.

Which worked-out examples makes it easier for students to understand the rule of proportion? Why?

...

The examples within this section illustrate two key ideas. Firstly, example-specific self-explanation prompts can be a targeted way for teachers to drive students' attention to the key principles underlying the problem-solving processes they are studying. Secondly, there are a variety of ways to support student explanations that sit along a continuum from more to less support: multiple-choice prompts, fill-in-the-blank prompts, free-response prompts.

The limitation of this approach, as with all concrete and specific instructional approaches, is that the benefits are less likely to transfer to new situations. If we ask students, 'Why did Harry subtract 80 from 180 degrees in his second line of working?', they're likely to better understand the sum of the angles within a triangle, but are unlikely to change their self-explanation behaviours in many other contexts. Further, creating example-specific prompts can require a lot of teacher time. It is for these reasons that we now turn our attention to general self-explanation prompts.

165. Hilbert, T.S., Renkl, A., Schworm, S., Kessler, S. & Reiss, K. (2008) Learning to teach with worked-out examples: A computer-based learning environment for teachers. *Journal of Computer-Assisted Learning*, 24, pp. 316–332.

General self-explanation prompts

Training students to self-explain spontaneously and in a variety of new situations is no mean feat, but research into self-explanation training hints at the fact that this might just be possible.[166] The reason that I say 'hint' is that, while generic self-explanation training has demonstrated learning gains in the short to medium term, research into whether self-explanation training can turn less- into more-successful learners over the long term remains to be undertaken.[167]

From the studies in which a general approach to teaching self-explanations has been successful, the approach follows a familiar pattern: tell students about the importance of self-explanations, provide them with some models of high quality self-explanations, then have them practice self-explaining some material.[168]

In reading through the generic self-explanation research, four prompt themes emerged as most promising. The studies that reported positive findings from a generic approach seemed to target process, connection, anticipation, or principles. Some examples are detailed below.

Process prompts

Process-oriented self-explanation prompts help students to interrogate their own understanding of a process or procedure. These are often used when students are studying a worked example, but they can also be used in other processes, such as reading.

One example of three useful process questions can be remembered with the steps, 'notice, reason, monitor'. They could look as follows.

- Notice: What parts of this page are new to me?

- Reason: How does this new piece of information help?

- Monitor: Is there anything I still don't understand?

Researchers who utilised these three questions in self-explanation training reported that, 'The results in this study reinforce the view that a self-explanation

---

166. Renkl, A., Solymosi, J., Erdmann, M. & Aleven, V. (2013) Training principle-based self-explanations: Transfer to new learning contents. In *Proceedings of the Annual Meeting of the Cognitive Science Society* (Vol. 35, No. 35).
167. Renkl, A. (2020) Personal communication, 2 June.
168. Renkl. R & Eitel. R. (2019) Self Explaining: Learning about Principles and Their Application, pp. 528-549 in Dunlosky, J. & Rawson, K.A. (Eds.) (2019) *The Cambridge Handbook of Cognition and Education. Cambridge*: Cambridge University Press.

procedure can be seen as a simple but potentially powerful technique for acquiring knowledge during study'.[169]

A similar set of questions, suggested by Alan Schoenfeldt,[170] could be more useful during the problem solving process:

- What exactly are you doing? Can you describe it precisely?

- Why are you doing it? How does it fit into the solution?

- How does it help you? What will you do with the outcome when you obtain it?

Connection prompts

Learning something new requires taking the new piece of information and connecting it in some meaningful way to an idea already stored in long-term memory. Some students do this more naturally than others, so it's beneficial to spend some time helping students to internalise questions that facilitate such connections. For students to connect new information to old, they need to learn to ask themselves questions such as:

- How are ... and ... similar?

- What is the difference between ... and ...?

- How does ... tie in with ... that we learned before?[171]

Anticipation prompts

Anticipation prompts strive to sow the seeds of transfer by having students consider what will happen next, either in the immediate future, or further down the track. In Renkl's 1997 study, in which he found that only one third of participants were effective self-explainers, a large portion of these effective self-explainers did so in an 'anticipatory' way.[172]

---

169. Wong, R.M., Lawson, M.J. & Keeves, J. (2002) The effects of self-explanation training on students' problem solving in high-school mathematics. *Learning and Instruction.* 12 (2), 233–262. p. 253,

170. Schoenfeld, A. H. (1985) *Mathematical problem solving.* New York: Academic Press. As referenced in Foster, C. (2019) *The fundamental problem with teaching problem solving.* Association of Teachers of Mathematics.

171. King, A. (1994) Guiding knowledge construction in the classroom: Effects of teaching children how to question and how to explain. *American Educational Research Journal.* 31 (2), 338–368. p. 345.

172. Renkl, A. (1997) Learning from worked-out examples: A study on individual differences. *Cognitive Science.* 21 (1), 1–29.

Anticipatory reasoning can be encouraged with two very simple questions:

- What will happen next?[173]

- What would happen if...?[174]

The former question is applicable to worked examples, in any reading task, or even during a teachers' explanation. As Marcia Heiman suggests, successful learners continually form hypotheses about what will happen next, whether in a lecture, conversation, or when reading. They then read on or listen on in order to check if their hypotheses were correct.[175]

I used to frequently use the second question, 'What would happen if?' with my friends at University. We would have competitions to try to guess the ways in which our lecturers may alter our assignment questions in order for them to write questions to be included in our exams. By asking, 'What would happen if?' we would end up exploring all manner of different scenarios and questions that we thought could be reasonably asked based upon the questions we'd already been given, and the principles that they exemplified. I now try to teach my own students to apply this question, and challenge them to guess the variations on class and homework problems I may use for an upcoming test!

Principle prompts

Perhaps the simplest generic prompt type is the principle prompt; students can simply be encouraged to consider for themselves:

- What principle was used here?

...

With all of the general self-explanation prompts presented above, the goal is that these questions become part of students' spontaneous internal dialogue. First the teacher introduces them explicitly, explains the types of situations in

---

173. Students were taught to consider what will happen in the following study: Renkl, A., Solymosi, J., Erdmann, M. & Aleven, V. (2013) Training principle-based self-explanations: Transfer to new learning contents. In Proceedings of the Annual Meeting of the Cognitive Science Society (Vol. 35, No. 35).

174. King, A. (1994) Guiding knowledge construction in the classroom: Effects of teaching children how to question and how to explain. *American Educational Research Journal.* 31 (2), 338–368. p. 345.

175. Heiman, M. (1987) Learning to learn: A behavioral approach to improving thinking. In D.N. Perkins, J. Lochhead & J. Bishop (Eds.) *Thinking: The Second International Conference* (pp. 431–452). Hillsdale, NJ: Lawrence Erlbaum Associates, Inc. p. 70. As cited Gray, P. (1993) Engaging students' intellects: The immersion approach to critical thinking in psychology instruction. *Teaching of Psychology,* 20(2), 68-74.

which each prompt is useful, then continues to reinforce them over time. Over a period of weeks and months, the teacher continues to ask the same questions as they circulate around the class. Students learn that when the teacher comes over, they're probably going to be asked the questions, so naturally begin to prepare answers themselves. Eventually, the self-explanation process becomes part of the students' internal dialogue, and the presence of the teacher is no longer required to trigger effective self-questioning and self-explanation in an appropriate situation. This process can also be supported by effective use of peer-questioning, and Socratic methods more generally.

Self-explanation prompts for teachers when reading education research

Self-explanations are helpful for teachers too. In order to gain a solid yet flexible understanding of educational principles and research, there are a few questions we can periodically ask ourselves. These include:

- What is the mechanism behind this instructional approach?[176]

- What is the function of this instructional approach?[177]

- What are the boundary conditions of this instructional approach?

Considering the mechanisms behind an approach helps us to understand *why* it works and what the active ingredients are. Without understanding what the mechanisms are, we risk adapting an approach in a way that misses its active ingredients, leading to a 'lethal mutation'.[178] Understanding the function is imperative, because to answer the question, 'What works best?' we must be able to add, 'For what purpose?' Functions tell us what an instructional approach can and can't do. Finally, boundary conditions are extra insurance against the misapplication of an approach. While mechanisms help us to see *why* an approach works, boundary conditions help us to know *why* not. Often boundary conditions can be anticipated if you already have a deep understanding of mechanisms, but it's always worth explicitly considering them, which is what we'll do for self-explanation now!

---

176. Lovell, O. Errr #017. Adrian Simpson Critiquing The Meta-Analysis. *Ollie Lovell Learning To Teach, Teaching To Learn* Available at: https://www.ollielovell.com/errr/adriansimpson/

177. Lovell, O. Errr #044. Alexander Renkl on Self-Explanation. *Ollie Lovell Learning To Teach, Teaching To Learn* Available at: https://www.ollielovell.com/errr/alexander-renkl-self-explanations

178. Brown, A.L. & Campione, J.C. (1996) *Psychological theory and the design of innovative learning environments: On procedures, principles, and systems.* New Jersey: Lawrence Erlbaum Associates, Inc.

The limits of self-explanation

While self-explanations are best placed in the early stages of learning, the act of self-explanation itself can overload working memory. This means that 'self-explanations only may be effective once a sufficient level of expertise has been attained'.[179] This is one of the reasons why some self-explanation studies have reported null results.[180]

Perhaps **the most insidious trap** associated with an attempted use of self-explanation prompts by teachers is the danger of **trying to have students teach themselves what they don't know**. Taken with the idea that students 'self-explaining' is a useful instructional strategy, teachers may ask students to self-explain before they have been taught the underlying principles. Self-explanation prompts are a method by which students can be encouraged to connect *previously* learned theory with a *new* set of examples. They are **not** designed for students to teach themselves the theory or principles in the first place (although self-explanation could be used to prompt students to consider a phenomenon they observe, perhaps in a science class, prior to being taught the principle explicitly).

It is also important to ask ourselves whether or not self-explanation prompts are *the best* way to achieve their goal. Principle-based self-explanation prompts are only one way of supporting students to connect specific examples to the principles underlying them,[181] and they can often take longer than simply telling students the connections you'd like to emphasise.[182] As McEldoon and colleagues state, 'attention needs to be paid to how much self-explanation offers advantages over alternative uses of time.'[183]

But it isn't simply a case of either self-explanations *or* explicit instruction. In fact, particularly promising findings come from studies in which the two are

---

179. Sweller, J., Ayres, P. & Kalyuga, S. (2011) *Cognitive Load Theory.* Vol. 1. New York: Springer New York. p. 189.
180. See, for example, Mwangi, W. & Sweller, J. (1998) Learning to solve compare word problems: The effect of example format and generating self-explanations. *Cognition and Instruction,* 16, 173–199.
181. Rittle-Johnson, B. & Loehr, A.M. (2017) Eliciting explanations: Constraints on when self-explanation aids learning. *Psychonomic Bulletin & Review,* 24(5), 1501–1510.
182. Bisra, K., Liu, Q., Nesbit, J.C., Salimi, F. & Winne, P.H. (2018) Inducing self-explanation: A meta-analysis. Educational Psychology Review. 30 (3), 703–725.
183. McEldoon, K.L., Durkin, K.L. & Rittle-Johnson, B. (2013) Is self-explanation worth the time? A comparison to additional practice. *British Journal of Educational Psychology.* 83 (4), 615–632. p. 1.

used in tandem. For example, one study[184] concluded that self-explanations were as effective as instructional explanations, but even larger gains were found when students were asked to self-explain first, and *then* prompted to compare their self-explanations with instructional explanations; as could be done in observing some phenomenon, hypothesising an explanation, then being taught the principle. If this approach is taken, ensure that students don't recognise this pattern, or they may 'check out' while being asked to self-explain, as they've learned they'll be told the explanation afterwards regardless of whether or not they engage in self-explanation.[185]

Even with all of these caveats, it still stands that **to learn from worked examples, students must interrogate and self-explain their understanding.** As such, self-explanation prompts are a powerful tool to enhance student learning.

The goal-free effect

When we set a problem for students to solve, there are two main things we want them to achieve. The most obvious of the two, and the objective that students are usually most aware of, is to obtain the correct answer. The less obvious to students, but far more important objective, is for the student to learn how to better solve other problems in future. The goal-free effect highlights the fact that, somewhat counterintuitively, these two objectives are often in tension.

The goal-free effect was the first cognitive load effect ever studied.[186] These early studies revealed two surprising results. Firstly, focusing on the most obvious goal (finding the right answer), often reduces the amount that students learn from the problem. Second, and more surprisingly, focusing on getting the right answer can also make students less likely to get the right answer!

But how could this be?

Put simply, when students focus on obtaining a fixed goal, their attention is directed at frequently checking where they are, how far away they are from the goal, and which next action is likely to get them closest to their desired

---

184. Cho, Y.H. & Jonassen, D.H. (2012) Learning by self-explaining causal diagrams in high-school biology. *Asia Pacific Education Review*, 13(1), 171–184.

185. Lovell, O. Errr #044. Alexander Renkl on Self-Explanation. *Ollie Lovell Learning To Teach, Teaching To Learn* Available at: https://www.ollielovell.com/errr/alexander-renkl-self-explanations/

186. Sweller, J. & Levine, M. (1982) Effects of goal specificity on means–ends analysis and learning. *Journal of Experimental Psychology: Learning, Memory, and Cognition.* 8 (5), 463.

end point; this is called means-ends analysis.[187] In cases for which there are multiple possible next steps – for example option a, b, or c – this means-ends analysis is a task very high in element interactivity. Removing the goal removes a large number of the interacting elements associated with means-ends analysis, freeing up working memory resources to focus on learning. This is the goal-free effect.

The goal-free effect: removing the goal removes a large number of the interacting elements associated with means-ends analysis, freeing up working memory resources to focus on learning.

Removing the goal also allows students to shift their focus from constantly measuring their progress, to a more experimental mindset in which they can take actions a, b, *and* c, and pay close attention to the results of those actions. From their close observations, they discover the outcome that each of these three actions generates.[188] This deeper understanding of cause and effect, action and outcome, puts students in a much stronger position to understand the current problem and to solve new problems in future.

These two mechanisms, reduced element interactivity, and a shift in focus from 'getting the answer' to cause and effect, are the proposed mechanisms behind the goal-free effect.

These two mechanisms, reduced element interactivity, and a shift in focus from 'getting the answer' to cause and effect, are the proposed mechanisms behind the goal-free effect.

But we can't just remove the goal from any task and expect the benefits of the goal-free effect to emerge. From within the dense literature on the goal-free effect I have uncovered and named the three key pre-conditions that underlie the vast majority of the successful research in this space. I call these three pre-conditions: **restricted actions**, **rapid feedback**, and **reliable results**.

Restricted actions are important within the goal-free effect because, if there are too many things students can do within a goal-free problem solving

---

187. Simon, D.P. & Simon, H.A. (1978) Individual differences in solving physics problems. In R. S. Siegler (Ed.), *Children's thinking: What develops?* (pp. 325–348). New Jersey: Lawrence Erlbaum.

188. Trumpower, D.L., Goldsmith, T.E. & Guynn, M. J. (2004) Goal specificity and knowledge acquisition in statistics problem solving: Evidence for attentional focus. *Memory & Cognition*, 32(8), 1379-1388.

environment, there will be too many action → outcome pairs for them to keep track of, and students' working memories will likely become overloaded.

Rapid feedback means students can very quickly see the impact of their actions. If there is a delay between students taking actions and observing outcomes, this splitting of attention will make it harder for them to recognise the connection between their actions and the outcomes that result.

Finally, **reliable results** means that if a student takes '*action* a', they can rely on the fact that they will get '*outcome* a'. If a student tries to use a formula, but makes an error and instead produces 'outcome %$#' (an unreliable result) then they stand little chance of learning the true connection between 'action a' and its result.

> **For a goal-free approach to be successful it must include: restricted actions, rapid feedback, and reliable results.**

These three pre-conditions explain the frequent use of digital learning environments within goal-free research. A digital learning environment enables the instructor to limit the number of possible actions, have results shown to students almost immediately, and perform calculations (and other behind-the-scenes work) to reliably show students the outcomes of their actions each time.

We will now examine how the goal-free effect could look, and has looked, in a range of different subjects.

The goal-free effect in physics

There are many simulations[189] available that allow physics students to see a clear representation of physical phenomena. In the past, it has been my general approach to use these to help demonstrate worked examples. That is, I would set a question using quantities from the simulation, have students predict the result through their calculations, then play the simulation to show it in action.

However, a goal-free study by Miller and colleagues[190] has made me doubt whether my existing method is the most powerful approach. In their study, students were given an opportunity to engage with a 'microworlds' simulator involving fixed and moving charged particles. Their task was to fix a set of charged particles along a course such that they would attract or repel a freely

---

189. Some particularly powerful simulators can be found at: https://phet.colorado.edu/, https://www.walter-fendt.de/html5/phen/, https://www.tinkercad.com/learn/circuits

190. Miller, C.S., Lehman, J.F. & Koedinger, K.R. (1999) Goals and learning in microworlds. *Cognitive science.* 23 (3), 305–336.

moving particle and successfully guide it towards a 'net' (see below. This goal 'net' is pictured rightmost as a backwards 'C' shape[191]).

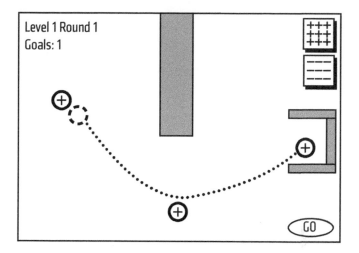

After an initial period in which both groups were introduced to the game, the *goal-specific* group was given 30 minutes to work through various levels of the game, such as the one pictured above. The *goal-free* group was given a blank screen with a set of fixed and movable particles that they could drag onto the screen themselves, along with the following instructions:

> *Later, you will be given a situation with obstacles and a net.*
>
> *For the next 30 minutes, however, you are asked to 'experiment' in a situation without any obstacles or a net. Your objective is to learn to understand the game's properties in any way you see fit.*
>
> *30 minutes may seem like a long time, but you should try to continue experimenting as much as possible during this time.*

In short, the *goal-specific* group was told to work through a series of levels, the *goal-free* group was told to experiment and understand.

After this experimental period, results demonstrated that encouraging students to 'experiment' with the programme allowed the goal-free group to better understand the fundamental interactions between the particles, and to do

191. Miller, C.S., Lehman, J.F. & Koedinger, K.R. (1999) Goals and learning in microworlds. *Cognitive science.* 23 (3), p. 308.

better than the goal-specific group in the final tests. This result was particularly pronounced for low-achieving students, and occurred despite the fact that the goal-specific group had spent their 30 minutes completing challenges very similar to the final assessment challenge.

This experiment has caused me to rethink how I use online physics simulations to teach physics. After a discussion of the fundamental physics principles, I now provide students with at least a short period with the simulator to 'experiment' and 'try to understand', prior to moving on to goal-specific tasks.

The goal-free effect in economics

One of the key skills within economics is understanding the ways in which changes to aggregate demand and aggregate supply of a product or service tend to influence price and quantity. Manipulating the supply and demand curves to represent this relationship is a task that many students struggle with.

The way this is usually taught is that students use pen and paper to shift the different functions, and are asked to describe the outcomes; a goal-specific approach. If a teacher wanted to trial a goal-free stance, they could instead stand at the board and ask students to direct *them* to move the supply and demand curves as the students see fit, to experiment, and to begin to discuss and record the results that they see (the teacher here provides the rapid actions and reliable results). Alternatively, students could be encouraged to use an online interactive graph[192] and given time to first explore cause and effect prior to receiving explicit instruction. Teachers could also design their own such activity through an interactive design programme.[193]

This approach should come after students have already received some instruction in the role, purpose, and interactions of the supply and demand functions, and as a precursor to students attempting goal-specific supply and demand problems themselves.

The goal-free effect in art

Quality art is produced at the intersection of conceptual and technical skill. The goal-free effect could be used to create a safe environment to develop the technical side of things. Instead of teaching students a set of brush techniques, and then have them immediately apply them to produce some predefined picture (a goal-specific approach) the teacher could first teach the techniques, and then set students free to play with these techniques, inviting them to pay

---

192. Examples of these can be found at https://www.econgraphs.org/
193. A great example of this can be found at https://www.desmos.com

close attention to the impact of slight variations in how each stroke is applied. The start, the finish, the weight, or other brush stroke variations the students could think up are likely to produce different effects they can readily observe. By experimenting with materials and techniques in this way – a method already used by many art teachers – students could come to better understand the connection between small variations in the actions they take, and the products of those actions, preparing them to more flexibly apply these techniques when the time comes to compose a coherent piece.

The goal-free effect in music

Rather than explicitly teaching intervals at the outset, such as major, minor, or diminished, students could be invited to play with various two note combinations and to try to get a sense of the emotions that each invokes. This could build a strong intuitive foundation for later formalisation of those same intervals.

The goal-free effect in history

Towards the end of the first burst of goal-free effect research, Vollmeyer and Burns[194] decided to extend the exploration of the effect beyond the algorithmic fields of physics and mathematics. They chose to home in on the type of online research assignment often given to students, such as 'Research the spread and impact of the black death throughout Europe' or 'Research the causes of World War I'.

Research assignments like this are often scaffolded by providing students with a set of questions they are to fill out while researching things like key historical figures, important battles or significant dates. But could these specific goals be getting in the way of learning?

The researchers set up the equivalent of a simple Wikipedia-like site that consisted of 51 pages, describing countries involved, alliances, nationalism, imperialism, and other events and individuals involved in the lead up to World War I. The goal-specific group was given a list of 20 events and asked to find the dates of each. The goal-free group was simply told to work through the programme, 'with the goal of explaining the outbreak of World War I to someone else.'[195]

194. Vollmeyer, R. & Burns, B.D. (2002) Goal specificity and learning with a hypermedia program. *Experimental psychology.* 49 (2), 98.
195. Vollmeyer, R. & Burns, B.D. (2002) Goal specificity and learning with a hypermedia program. *Experimental psychology.* 49 (2), 98. p. 101.

Each group was given 25 minutes to explore the programme and at the end of it were presented with a collection of test questions: 34 factual questions, one question on the main reason that five countries declared war on each other during the period of a week, and a transfer question relating to alliance formation between four tribes. When students were tested, the goal-free group did significantly better than the goal-specific group on all types of questions. They also spent more time on each page than the goal-specific group, indicating deeper consideration and processing of the information therein.

In this context, providing students with the space to explore the mechanisms underlying the lead up to the war, rather than focusing them on a list of specific facts and figures to find out, led to a much broader and deeper understanding. While this experiment shows that in some cases, more general instructions to 'understand' and 'explain to someone else' can lead to more learning than following specific instructions, it's also important to note the likely role of both competence and motivation on the efficacy of this approach. The subjects in this experiment were university students and likely motivated by the public sharing of their learning at the end. A similar level of research competency, background knowledge, and motivation may be required for a similarly successful outcome in another setting.

The goal-free effect in biology

Biologists often look at how environmental factors influence the populations of various species within their environments. One goal-free effect study targeted such a set of relationships, in this case, the impact of four environmental factors (temperature, salt, oxygen, and current) on the populations of four marine species (prawns, sea bass, lobster, and crab) within a computer-based simulation.

A goal-specific group was told that their ultimate objective was to manipulate the four environmental factors to achieve final populations of 400 prawns, 700 sea bass, 900 lobsters, and 50 crabs. They were given three practice rounds to work out how to do this, with each round consisting of six consecutive opportunities to change the four environmental factors. The goal-free group, on the other hand, was told to simply 'set inputs and observe outputs in order to figure out how the system works'. [196]

Three test rounds were undertaken for both goal-specific and goal-free groups. In the fourth round, all students were required to manipulate the environmental

---

196. Vollmeyer, R., Burns, B.D. & Holyoak, K.J. (1996) The impact of goal specificity on strategy use and the acquisition of problem structure. *Cognitive Science*, 20(1), 75–100. p. 89.

factors to achieve 400 prawns, 700 sea bass, 900 lobsters, and 50 crabs; the same outcome that had been targeted by the goal-specific group during practice.

Surprisingly, the goal-free group did *just* as well on this test problem as the goal-specific group, even though the goal-specific group had been working on exactly the same problem for the prior three rounds!

Round five was a transfer round, in which students were required to get the system to 200 prawns, 350 sea bass, 1000 lobsters, and 250 crabs, a new goal for both groups. On this transfer problem, the goal-free group did significantly better than the goal-specific group. The goal-free group had discovered the relationships between the four input factors, and increases or decreases in the populations of the marine animals. In this way, the goal-free approach had achieved both objectives; goal-free students were able to successfully solve the problems, *and* they'd learned how to solve similar problems in future.

The goal-free effect in mathematics

Students often mix up the trigonometric ratios of sin, cos, and tan, applying them in a trial-and-error-like fashion, without ever really understanding their proper use. In one of the most impressive goal-free studies to date, Owen and Sweller[197] targeted these three ratios to see if a goal-free approach could help students to not only understand their basic use, but to develop deep conceptual understanding they could transfer to an unfamiliar problem.

They started off providing six worked examples to the participants (a group of Year 9 students), each demonstrating the calculation of the numerator and the denominator within a sin, cos, or tan equation respectively. Throughout this practice, students were required to perform related calculations and, once they could produce reliable results, the goal-free and goal-specific conditions commenced.

Students were given 30 minutes to work with combinations of triangles such as the two pictured below:[198]

197. Owen, E. & Sweller, J. (1985) What do students learn while solving mathematics problems? *Journal of Educational Psychology.* 77 (3), 272. Note: Experiment three from that study is described herein.
198. ibid. pp. 275 and 279.

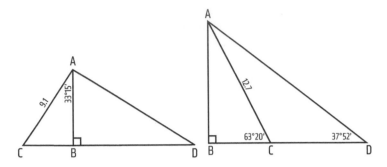

Goal-specific participants were told to find a specific side, for example 'Find side AD in the leftmost triangle above', whereas the goal-free group were simply invited to 'Find the length of all unknown sides'. During this phase the students had a researcher next to them and, whenever they made a trigonometric mistake, the researcher would simply highlight that they'd made an error in applying one of the formulas, without telling them what that error was (remember the importance of reliable results).

At the end of this 30-minute practice phase, students were given the following transfer problem.

In a certain triangle, sin(θ) = $\frac{4}{5}$ and cos(θ) = $\frac{3}{5}$. Draw a diagram to illustrate this, and hence find the value of tan(θ).

Now, as maths teachers will know, this is a very tricky problem for Year 9 students who have only had 30 minutes of practice with sin, cos, and tan.

Incredibly, 80% in the goal-free group were able to solve this problem, compared to 30% of the goal-specific group. Further, the goal-specific group made more than twice as many errors as the goal-free group when trying to solve the problem. This large number of errors by the goal-specific group indicated that they were 'unable to interpret in a meaningful way the information given in the question';[199] that is to say that even though 30% of them did get the answer to this transfer problem, guessing played a significant role in their success (students were allowed multiple attempts).

To me, these results are truly remarkable. To get 80% of students from no knowledge of trigonometry to solving a transfer problem like this within a practice period of only 30 minutes is very impressive. But we must keep in mind

199. Owen, E. & Sweller, J. (1985) What do students learn while solving mathematics problems? *Journal of Educational Psychology*, 77(3), 272. p. 282.

the goal-free prerequisites. If classroom application of this approach doesn't allow for rapid feedback when students are applying the trigonometric ratios (as was provided in this study), this approach is unlikely to be as successful. This is why appropriate technology is such a powerful tool to provide the rapid feedback and reliable results required to facilitate effective use of the goal-free effect.

For those wanting deeper insight into the vastly increased cognitive load that results from a goal-specific approach in this context, the following diagrams communicate the number of interacting elements at one time point of the goal-free versus goal-specific version of this trigonometry activity.

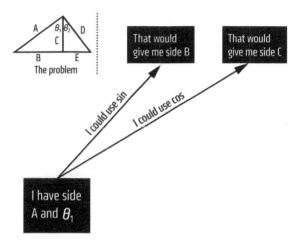

Interacting elements when considering the first two possible steps of this goal-free problem

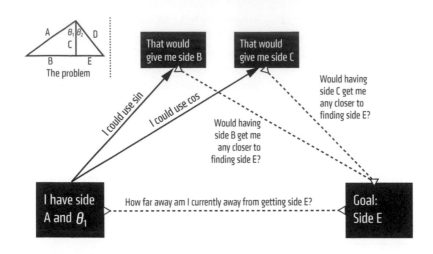

Interacting elements when considering the first two possible steps of this goal-specific problem

The goal-free effect when reading education research

Let's now take a step back to explore what it could look like to apply this goal-free finding from education research to the practice of reading education research!

A goal-specific approach: the reader looks specifically for facts, figures, quotes, or diagrams that provide evidence for a certain thesis.

A goal-free approach: the reader *explores* the literature with no specific goal in mind other than to fully understand the actions the experimenters took and the outcomes these actions generated.

It is only by taking this second approach, reading with an inquisitive mindset, searching for cause and effect, actions and outcomes, that we can come to a true understanding of the mechanisms underlying the studies we read; it is the only way to come to an understanding of how learning happens. Further, it is only by understanding the mechanisms behind learning that we can flexibly come up with new instructional approaches that have a high probability of benefitting our students. I strongly encourage you to take a goal-free approach to reading education research where possible.

The goal-free effect: what's the big idea?

An excessive focus on goals can lead to students successfully completing a task, but learning very little from it. This is the big idea of the goal-free effect.

It applies when attempting to learn from problem solving, but it also applies in many other facets of learning and life too. We've now seen how this can occur in a variety of situations. Within each, a focus upon getting the right answer drives both attention, and cognitive resources, away from the actual process of learning.

The big idea of the goal-free effect: an excessive focus on goals can lead to students successfully completing a task, but learning very little from it.

For Dylan Wiliam, this is the big idea of Cognitive Load Theory, and the reason he suggested that 'Cognitive Load Theory is the single most important thing for teachers to know'. Dylan put it as follows in a discussion I had with him:

> *For me, the reason that CLT is important for teachers to know about is that most teachers assume that if students satisfactorily complete an instructional activity, they will learn what that task is designed to teach them. CLT shows this is not true.*[200]

This is an immensely important result for teachers to be aware of. Thankfully, the recommendations of the goal-free effect don't just stop there. They also tell us that removing the goal – and doing so under conditions in which students have restricted actions, rapid feedback, and reliable results – can help the focus shift from 'getting the right answer' to 'learning'.

It may be tempting to think that simply *knowing* about the negative impact that specific goals can have on learning will be sufficient to stop their negative effects. Not so, and this is perhaps what has most shocked me in my exploration of the goal-free effect. That is, goals drive people away from a learning focus, *even when they know they should be focusing on learning.*

Goals drive people away from a learning focus, even when they know they should be focusing on learning.

This was clearly illustrated in Vollmeyer and colleagues' biology study[201] (crabs, lobsters, and sea bass, mentioned above). In this study, the optimum approach to working out how animal populations were influenced by the four environmental factors (temperature, salt, oxygen, and current) was to take a truly scientific approach, to vary one factor at a time, observe its impact on the

---

200. Wiliam, D. (2020) Personal communication, 13 July.
201. Vollmeyer, R., Burns, B.D. & Holyoak, K.J. (1996) The impact of goal specificity on strategy use and the acquisition of problem structure. *Cognitive Science*, 20(1), 75–100. p. 89.

system, and do so until the impact of each individual factor on the system could be understood in isolation.

What I didn't mention in my initial description of this biology experiment is that half of each group, goal-free and goal-specific, were *explicitly* told that 'vary one factor at a time' was the optimum learning strategy, and the best way to both solve the problem (get to a target number of each species), and learn how the system truly worked. The goal-free students, by and large, took this approach and applied the 'vary one thing at a time' strategy consistently throughout the three learning rounds. They were free to do so as they weren't pressured by knowledge of a defined goal.

But for the goal-specific group who had been told that the 'vary one thing at a time' strategy was optimal, most attempted it for only the first round, but quickly abandoned it in favour of a 'change many things at a time' strategy. This 'change many things' strategy helped them get to the final pre-defined end point, but as we saw, it meant they learned little, and were ill prepared to face a slightly modified problem within entirely the same environment in the future. Even though they were explicitly told how to best achieve both important goals – attaining the correct answer and actually learning from the problem – the mere presence of a goal drove them towards a shallow, goal-focused strategy which compromised their learning.

In the classroom, and education more broadly, we must be careful of the ways in which goals influence our students' approaches to learning tasks. How does marking whether homework is 'finished' or not push students to pursue unhelpful strategies like copying from friends? How do we unwittingly emphasise the importance of students getting the right answer rather than reflecting on and learning from the thinking processes that were used to obtain it? How does a focus on ticking the boxes of the rubric constrain the creativity of our students' writing? This is the big idea of the goal free effect: **an excessive focus on goals can lead to students successfully completing a task, but learning very little from it.**

CONCLUSIONS
COGNITIVE LOAD THEORY, WHERE TO FROM HERE?

The aim of this book has been to summarise Cognitive Load Theory in a clear and actionable way. I have tried to provide practical examples of *how* to apply Cognitive Load Theory, along with guidance around *why* these cognitive load effects work. This combination of practical guidance, and an explanation of mechanisms, hopefully means that you, the reader, now feel able to use the strategies presented, understand their limitations, and have a clear idea of how to effectively adapt them to your local context.

While the preceding chapters have focused on the well-established and experimentally-supported cognitive load effects already within the literature. In this final chapter, I would like to turn an eye to the future, and paint a picture of what I see as some of the most promising avenues for research ahead.

We began this book with the story of how a tweet by Dylan Wiliam catapulted me into an exploration of Cognitive Load Theory. I described how Cognitive Load Theory gave me a deeper understanding of my students' learning, and shone a light onto the inner workings of their minds, helping me to better understand what was holding them back in some of my lessons, and what enabled learning in others.

But the seeds of this interest started long before I was trying to improve my *teaching*. Instead, they started during a time in which I was intently focused on becoming a better *learner*.

I read Daniel Willingham's *Why Don't Students Like School*[202] during the final year of my undergraduate degree, and it had the single biggest impact on my life of any book up to that point. Willingham's book was life-changing for me because it taught me about the *cognitive architecture* underlying my own learning processes, the same cognitive architecture on which Cognitive Load Theory is built.

---

202. Willingham, D.T. (2009) *Why don't students like school? A cognitive scientist answers questions about how the mind works and what it means for the classroom.* New Jersey: John Wiley & Sons.

Before this revelation, I had focused upon organising my learning in the external world; taking good notes, making good summaries, and finding out the best technology possible to file and order my learning resources. After I learned that deep knowledge in long-term memory is the true pathway to higher-order thinking, I immediately changed tack. I began to explore how to increase my internal knowledge store, using learning software such as Anki,[203] and more recently Dendro,[204] to build and retain long-term memories. This represented a complete shift in the focus of my learning; a shift from *information management* in notebooks and on computers, to *knowledge management* within my own long-term memory.

I was immediately, and forever, changed as a learner, and it was learning about how my own brain works that generated this seismic shift. Cognitive Load Theory has immense power to help teachers to better support student learning. That is the focus of this book. Looking forward, I believe the next frontier for the theory lies in supporting *students* to utilise Cognitive Load Theory to become more successful and independent learners.

Using Cognitive Load Theory to empower learners is important for several reasons. Firstly, there is great potential in its promise to help create more independent learners. Secondly, in any group of students we teach, we will inevitably encounter a large range of abilities. This means that what is 'optimised' instruction for one student won't be optimised for another. Third, it is becoming increasingly clear that cognitive load is not just a function of prior knowledge, element interactivity, and instructional organisation. It is also dependent upon how the learner *approaches* their learning.

To this third point, consider the fact that there is an infinite source of extraneous load available to *all* students at *all* times. That is, they can simply choose to daydream or engage in other off-task thinking rather than focusing on the task the teacher has set. Non-strategic daydreaming (in contrast to beneficial mental breaks) constitutes a focus on information that is wholly extraneous to the learning task at hand, and teachers have very limited power to prevent it. Given this, it's clear that an individual's motivation and self-control plays an important role in the total cognitive load they experience.[205] Off-task thinking represents a way in which student choices can lead to increased extraneous load from the teacher's point of view. But students can also be taught strategies that reduce their extraneous load.

---

203. More information about Anki can be found at: https://apps.ankiweb.net/
204. More information about Dendro can be found at: www.dendro.cloud
205. Eitel. A., Endres, T. & Renkl, A. (in press), Self-Management as a Bridge between Cognitive Load and Self-Regulated Learning: The Illustrative Case of Seductive Details. *Education Psychology Review.*

This is an area of research gaining increasing attention at present, with several studies demonstrating that teaching students about cognitive load effects can help them to learn more effectively, even from materials that are poorly designed. The beneficial impact of teaching students how to better manage their own cognitive load has been termed the 'self-management effect'.[206]

Self-management of cognitive load effects: the research

Split-attention: Studies have presented students with learning materials that induce split-attention, but also taught these students how to reduce split-attention themselves. These studies have demonstrated that when students are taught about how to reduce split-attention for themselves, they can independently integrate learning materials, and enhance their learning. The benefits of this self-management training also transferred to new learning materials.[207]

Redundancy: Another study taught some students to identify and ignore redundant information when learning about lightning storms, finding that these students were able to ignore redundant information, and therefore learn more than a control group.[208] Yet another study, this time with primary school students, demonstrated that teaching students to categorise information as relevant or irrelevant, and then to study only the relevant information, yielded similar benefits to receiving pre-prepared, redundancy-free resources, and was better than having redundancy-free resources in a far-transfer task. The authors concluded that 'teaching learners to remove redundant information provides similar benefits as instructor managed materials.'[209]

Research in this area is very much in its early stages, but there are many more options for the extension of this work. I sketch out some such ideas in the following section.

---

206. Mirza, F., Agostinho, S., Tindall-Ford, S., Paas, F. & Chandler, P. (2020) Self-management of cognitive load: Potential and challenges. In S. Tindall-Ford, S. Agostinho, and J. Sweller (Eds.), *Advances in Cognitive Load Theory* (pp. 157-167). New York: Routledge.

207. See Roodenrys, K., Agostinho, S., Roodenrys, S. & Chandler, P. (2012) Managing one's own cognitive load when evidence of split attention is present. *Applied Cognitive Psychology*, 26, 878-886. And Sithole, S., Chandler, P., Abeysekera, I. & Paas, F. (2017) Benefits of guided self-management of attention on learning accounting. *Journal of Educational Psychology*, 109(2), 220-232.

208. Eitel, A., Bender, L. & Renkl, A. (2019) Are seductive details seductive only when you think they are relevant? An experimental test of the moderating role of perceived relevance. *Applied Cognitive Psychology*, 33(1), 20–30.

209. Mirza, F., Agostinho, S., Tindall-Ford, S., Paas, F. & Chandler, P. (2020) Self-management of cognitive load: Potential and challenges. In S. Tindall-Ford, S. Agostinho, and J. Sweller (Eds.), *Advances in Cognitive Load Theory* (pp. 157-167). New York: Routledge. p. 161.

Self-management of cognitive load effects: some ideas

In an attempt to illustrate some future paths for research in this area, I've compiled the following list of interesting avenues of exploration that could possibly support students to become more effective learners. Within these sketches, I share some of my own similar experiences in order to illustrate how they've helped me as a learner, and may therefore hold promise for our students too.

Pre-teaching: We could teach students about the relationship between long-term and working memory and therefore help them to understand the importance of prior knowledge. This could help motivate them to complete their pre-reading, to try harder to build and retain lasting knowledge, or to help them to ask teachers for relevant vocabulary (or search a textbook chapter for new vocabulary), prior to lessons. As mentioned, knowledge of my own memory system is what prompted me to fundamentally change my own approach to learning from *information management to knowledge management*. Interestingly, this shifted focus is reflected in my approach to researching Cognitive Load Theory itself. Whilst striving to master the research base for this book, I used the learning technology Dendro[210] to read, re-read, break down, compare, and space my study of the relevant literature. This approach provided a Cognitive Load Theory-aligned way for my brain to encounter the key ideas within the literature, and integrate them into my own long-term memory, making the learning process immeasurably more effective, enjoyable, and stress-free throughout. I see no reason why students couldn't use similar knowledge of their own memory system, or technology designed in line with it, to more quickly and effectively master knowledge they find interesting.

Isolated elements (manipulate the emphasis): We could teach students that when they're finding a task too difficult, they shouldn't focus on trying to do everything at once, but instead focus on one thing at a time. In this way, they could self-manage the learning of tasks that would be far too complex to learn in their entirety in one go. I do this with language learning. I am currently learning German, and I am paying very little attention to grammar and instead

---

210. In 2019 I met George Zonnios. At the time, George had begun developing the learning software Dendro (www.dendro.cloud), with the aim in mind of using research-informed principles to create a technology that supports people to learn more effectively and enjoyably. I immediately saw the promise in Dendro and have since joined George in its design and development (you can hear one of our early discussions at https://www.ollielovell.com/errr/ andymatuschakgeorgezonnios/). This is the first book ever written with the aid of Dendro, and we hope there will be many more to come! Our mission is to empower individuals and teams to be more productive in their self-directed learning.

focusing primarily on communicating ideas. This is the same approach I took to Mandarin learning, and in both cases it has acted as a fantastic way to reduce the number of interacting elements in the early stages of learning.

Redundancy: When students learn that receiving the same information in spoken words and writing at the same time causes interference within their working memory, they can choose to selectively engage with one or the other sources of information. Since learning about this form of redundancy, I have started to do this myself. If I notice that a presenter is speaking and showing similar words on their slides, I now simply watch the presenter and listen, eliminating the visually redundant written words, and also enjoying the presentations a lot more in the process!

Transient information: When I was studying physics at university, my friends and I would often come across a hard assignment problem, then visit the lecturer during office hours for help. In doing this, I noticed a pattern: we'd go into their office, ask a question, they'd explain it, we'd understand, then as soon as we stepped out of their office, we'd immediately forget what they'd said! I learned from this that the transience of the lecturer's explanation could be counteracted by pulling out my mobile phone and asking to record their explanation. More recently, I've also started recording my language exchanges, listening back to them, then turning them into digital flashcards.[211] We could similarly teach students that, when faced with transient information and high element interactivity, they should seek to record the instruction in some way, in order to overcome the transience of the information.

Worked examples: We could simply teach students that, 'when you're stuck, look for a worked example'. As teachers are aware, this is something that more successful learners often already know to do, but doesn't seem to occur for many less-successful learners. If students know that they should, and can, seek out worked examples, this could help to accelerate their learning.

The goal-free effect: I proposed a self-managed goal-free approach to John Sweller during our interview back in 2017.

> *OL: I was wondering if you think it would be at all possible to teach learners to turn problems from goal-specific problems to goal-free problems themselves? For example, perhaps we could conceptualise a general problem solving strategy as: 'If you don't think you can do the problem,*

---

211. You can find a tutorial of how I quickly and easily turn the recordings from my language exchanges into digital flashcards here: https://www.ollielovell.com/ollielearns/make-most-language-exchange-anki-cards/

what you should start doing is to just find stuff out'. Then say, 'Every five or ten minutes, if you see you've worked some stuff out, you should look back, and think about where you were trying to get to in the first place. If you can see how to get there, great. If you can't, just keep playing around and find some more stuff out.'

JS: That's smart. We haven't done that, but it ought to be done. Good idea. You should try it out. Yeah, I can't see anything but positives to that.[212]

Another application of self-management of the goal-free effect is helping learners to understand that 'An excessive focus on goals can lead to people successfully completing a task, but learning very little from it.' This is a principle I realised I could apply during the writing of this book. I had initially planned out a timeline for finishing each chapter, but I found the time-bound goal for each chapter was causing me to focus more on finishing on time, and writing quickly, rather than thorough research and thoughtful writing. Once I realised this, I immediately abandoned my time-bound goals, and instead focused upon the research and writing *process*, which helped me to relax, enjoy it more, and has hopefully produced a better final product.

As can be seen, there exist many promising avenues of future research regarding a self-management approach to Cognitive Load Theory. No matter how hard we as teachers strive to optimise instruction for our students, there will always be obstacles in the way. Students may *choose* to daydream, there may be a mix of student abilities in the class, or they may go to another teacher's class, another school, or onto higher education in which the instructor doesn't have the same knowledge of instructional principles that you now have after reading this book. Given this, one of the best gifts we can leave our students with is a toolset they can use to enhance their learning in any learning environment in the future.

But I thought you can't teach domain-general, biologically primary knowledge?

Within the 'ABCDE of CLT' in Part I, it was suggested that many proponents of Cognitive Load Theory do not believe that biologically primary knowledge, nor domain-general skills, can be taught. For some, this may appear to be at odds with the recommendations of this final chapter thus far. Didn't we evolve to self-manage ourselves? Don't humans come 'out of the box' ready to learn?

---

212. Lovell, O. (2017) John Sweller Interview 2: Can We Teach Problem Solving? *Ollie Lovell, Learning to Teach, Teaching to Learn.* Available at: https://www.ollielovell.com/pedagogy/johnsweller2/. This idea is yet to be tested, an area for future exploration!

Therefore, aren't 'self-management' and 'learning' biologically primary skills and, according to Cognitive Load Theory, we shouldn't be able to teach them? How can we resolve what seems to be a puzzling paradox?

After much reading and thinking, I presented this perceived paradox, and some ideas I had for its resolution, to John Sweller. Unsurprisingly, John had thought about this issue himself and was immediately able to produce a suggested resolution; there is no paradox! John argued that although both learning and self-management *are* biologically primary skills, Cognitive Load Theory is not; we did not evolve to learn about this theory and its effects. As such, while teaching students about split-attention may help with the biologically *primary* skill of self-regulated learning (as suggested in this chapter), we are not teaching self-regulated learning directly, rather, we are teaching students biologically *secondary* knowledge of the split-attention effect.[213] This is akin to the way in which increased domain-specific, biologically secondary knowledge is the pathway to helping people to improve in the biologically primary domain of problem solving. As such, the key message from this final chapter is enabled to come more fully to the fore. **Cognitive Load Theory is not only powerful in the hands of teachers** – as has hopefully been demonstrated through this book – **it is also powerful in the hands of learners**!

Cognitive Load Theory is not only powerful in the hands of teachers, it is also powerful in the hands of learners!

One final point on the teachability of biologically primary and domain-general skills before closing this section. Although several proponents of Cognitive Load Theory suggest that biologically primary and domain-general skills can't be *taught*, they do not in any way suggest that these skills cannot be *cultivated*. In the same discussion referred to above, John added the following:

> *Let's assume a child is born and physically looked after but was never talked to at all. Will that child learn to listen and speak? Obviously not. Just because we have evolved to acquire a skill doesn't mean that we will acquire it no matter what the circumstances. Nor does it mean we can't always improve the conditions.*[214]

That is, while several prominent Cognitive Load Theory researchers assert that we can't teach biologically primary skills, they don't argue that we can't improve *conditions* such that biologically primary skills can be developed more fully. A

---

213. Sweller, J. (2020) Personal correspondence, 5 July.
214. Sweller, J. (2020) Personal correspondence, 5 July.

good example of this is the way in which richer conversational environments provided by parents lead to enhanced language skills in their children.[215]

By way of analogy, although we can't *teach* a seedling to 'grow', we can ensure it has access to rich and fertile soil, and thereby enhance the chances that it can achieve the full measure of its innate, biologically primary potential. These enhanced conditions could even include programmes within schools specifically aimed at providing opportunities for students to develop these skills within an appropriately supportive environment.[216]

Cognitive Load Theory: What do you think?

I hope that this book has acted as a window into the potential of Cognitive Load Theory to improve your teaching. I hope you now better understand the mechanisms underlying learning and feel empowered to instruct your students with greater clarity, effectiveness, and confidence than you did before. And I hope this book also acts as a springboard for you to explore more education research in the future, and perhaps even conduct research into some of these exciting areas yourself!

Finally, I hope you're now better equipped to consider for yourself the Dylan Wiliam quote with which we began this book. Do you agree that *'Sweller's Cognitive Load Theory is the single most important thing for teachers to know'?*[217] I'd love to know what you think![218]

215. Romeo, R.R., Leonard, J.A., Robinson, S.T., West, M.R., Mackey, A.P., Rowe, M.L. & Gabrieli, J.D. (2018) Beyond the 30-million-word gap: Children's conversational exposure is associated with language-related brain function. *Psychological Science.* 29 (5), 700–710. p. 707.

216. See *Fear is the Mind Killer* by James Mannion and Kate McAllister for detailed guidance on some such programs and initiatives.

217. Wiliam, D. (2017) *I've come to the conclusion Sweller's Cognitive Load Theory is the single most important thing for teachers to know* (Twitter) 27 January. Available at: https://twitter.com/dylanwiliam/status/824682504602943489?lang=en

218. I always welcome questions, comments, thoughts and reflections from readers. You can reach me at ollie@ollielovell.com